Pulling a F...

Roger Protz

# Pulling a Fast One

### What the Brewers Have Done to Your Beer

Pluto  Press

First published 1978 by Pluto Press Limited
Unit 10 Spencer Court, 7 Chalcot Road, London NW1 8LH

Copyright © Pluto Press 1978

ISBN 0 86104 024 4

Text designed by Tom Sullivan
Text drawings by Stewart Walton
Maps by Joyce Batey
Cover illustration by Vince Farrell

Typeset by Red Lion Setters, Holborn, London
Printed in Great Britain by Cox & Wyman Ltd,
London, Fakenham and Reading

# Contents

# Acknowledgements

This book would not have been possible without the pioneering journalism of Michael Hardman, Christopher Hutt and Richard Boston, and the technical expertise of Stephen Foster. My thanks, too, to the Monopolies Committee of CAMRA for the painstaking research they have conducted in many parts of the country and to Fred Pearce of CAMRA's publications, whose careful analyses of Bass Charrington, Norfolk and the tied house system have made life easier for me. It must be stressed that the Campaign for Real Ale is in no way responsible for any of the conclusions of the book, which are mine alone. I am grateful to James Lynch, CAMRA chairman 1976-77, for permission to use material previously published in *What's Brewing*. Special thanks are due to Christopher Hird who read the manuscript and made many invaluable corrections and suggestions. Young & Co of Wandsworth generously allowed Stewart Walton to sketch in their brewery.

# Distribution of breweries in Britain in 1955

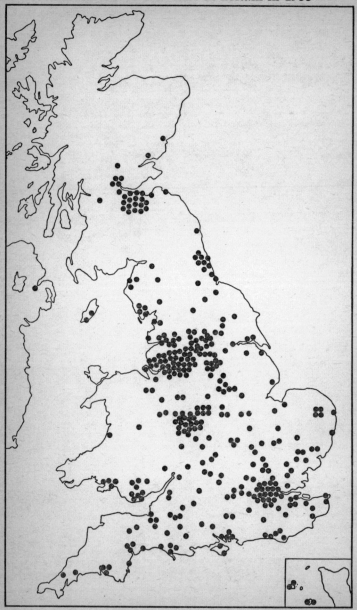

# Distribution of breweries in Britain in 1978

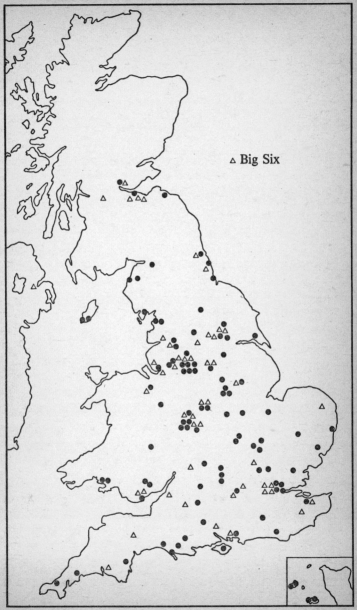

△ Big Six

# 1.

# Opening time

*'Just look at the breweries South Wales has lost over the years ... There were the Taff Vale and Giles and Harrop which kept the Merthyr Tydfil areas bubbling. Over the mountain the Black Lion slaked the thirsts of Aberdare. Then we had Evan Evans Bevan rolling out the barrels at Neath and in Mid-Glamorgan the Bridgend Brewery was kept busy keeping everyone's pints foaming. Also in a glass of their own at Cardiff were the redoubtable Hancocks and Ely breweries. Sparkling up at Aberbeeg were Webb's, while Phillips and Lloyd and Yorath of Newport kept a cool head in South Gwent. Now Brains of Cardiff, Felinfoel Ales and Buckleys of Llanelli are the sole remaining independent brews left in South Wales'* — Terry Campbell, South Wales Echo, *October 1977*

Thirty-two million pints of beer are drunk every day in Britain. Put another way, for every adult in the country, an average of nearly 30 gallons of beer are consumed every year. Production runs at more than 11,500 million pints a year. They are, in every sense of the word, staggering statistics.

Beer drinking is a national pastime, a highly-developed social activity and a source of endless debate. It is also big business. Sales from brewing, wholesaling and tied estates are running at about £2,861 million a year. The top six brewing companies make a combined annual profit of more than £300 million and the government creams off more than £1,100 million

11

in excise duty and VAT. A total of 825,000 people are engaged in malting, brewing, distributing and selling beer.

Ten million people use Britain's 66,000 pubs every day. While pubs are responsible for 60 per cent of beer sales, club and supermarket sales are growing fast.

All of these figures - the millions of pints drunk, the millions of pounds earned, the millions who drink and the large work-force kept in employment as a result of it all - should add up to one thing: pleasure.

But the pleasure is in short supply. There is something badly wrong with the brewing industry. In less than 20 years it has been transformed from an industry where several hundred regional companies produced a wide range of beers to suit every palate to an industry where six conglomerates dominate more than 80 per cent of production and supply. The number of beers available has been more than halved and the way in which beer is brewed and served has been revolutionised, to the detriment of its flavour and the consumers' taste-buds and pockets. Processed, sterile keg beers and lager, which accounted for a tiny sector of the market 20 years ago, now dominate, and traditional draught beer - the great ales of Britain, famous for their quality and variety - seemed in the early 1970s destined to become merely part of the history of brewing.

We have all come across the old man in the corner seat of the public bar who holds up his pint and mournfully tells the world that beer isn't what it used to be. Don't dismiss him as a crank in his dotage: the chances are that he is right, and is not glorifying the past with boozy hindsight. 'Progress' in brewing, as with so much of the progress that is left to vast industrial and commercial bureaucracies, has not benefited consumers. Most of the beer now drunk in Britain's pubs is weak, gassy and expensive, much of it totally dead and often carted around the country in enormous road tankers as if it were petrol or industrial waste. It is brewed - manufactured would be a better word - by chemists who have replaced the old brewing craftsmen and whose concern is not with quality but to meet the demands of the marketing men and the accountants who employ them. The tragedy is that a generation of young drinkers are being reared on mass-produced fizzy pap, or 'maltade' as one critic has called keg beer. Many have never tasted good, traditional beer, while older drinkers shrug and feel that they have to accept what is offered them.

The public houses are changing, too. The same 'Big Six' brewers - Bass Charrington, Allied Breweries, Watney Mann & Truman, Courage, Whitbread and Scottish and Newcastle - who have a stranglehold on beer also own more than half the pubs in which we drink. Their monopoly grip, which almost killed traditional beer, also threatens to wipe out that unique institution - the pub, the boozer, the local, the ale-house. Several hundred are closed every year as the brewers shut 'uneconomic' houses, mainly in rural areas, but also in the towns.

The word 'pub' is used so casually that we have forgotten its origin. The British pub is unique because it is a 'public house'. Unlike the cafes and bars of other countries, the British publican does not treat beer as a sideline, badgering his customers to buy coffee, newspapers and groceries. British beer drinkers, as the slogan suggested, are only there for the beer, in a pleasant, cheerful atmosphere.

The public house is an important part of the social fabric of the country. As the industrial revolution herded people off the land and into the towns, often to live in misery and squalor in the new slums, pubs were important havens for working people, a nicer place to be than your own 'home'. Society has moved on, but pubs still offer a warm place away from the many stresses of modern life, where you can down a few pints, strike up a conversation, play darts or dominoes or just quietly read a newspaper. The pub is a vital part of the local community: it organises football, cricket and darts teams; loan clubs are run from pubs and they often provide meeting places for social, political or trade union organisations, the chairmen and women of which have to run meetings with iron precision in order that proceedings end a good twenty minutes before the landlord calls 'time'.

Of course, there are many nasty pubs: sprawling, run-down city boozers where the staff glare belligerently at the unwary intruder; tarted-up plastic palaces, full of flashing neon lights and topless go-go dancers; tiny country pubs where the landlord and the locals make it clear that 'foreigners' are not

13

welcome. But they are fortunately rare, and a trip to the local usually remains a cheering activity.

But as with the beer, all is not well with the pub. While the brewers' real estate men go about their business of closure, sometimes even evicting landlords and their families, trendy young architects are also ruthlessly engaged in the business of 'modernisation'. The regular users of street-corner locals find to their horror that their pub has been re-designed as a large pineapple, a sputnik or a Wild West saloon to attract the gin-and-tonic and lager-and-lime trade. Public bars are ripped out and replaced by lounges with soft lights, soft carpets, wet-look mock leather - and several pennies on the price of a pint.

This assault on our beer and our pubs went mainly unchecked in the 1960s and early 1970s. Some drinkers were so distressed by the vandalism of the big brewers that they made the supreme sacrifice and gave up drinking. I didn't go quite as far, but came near to it. When I was a young journalist I soon learned the pleasures of the many pubs in the Fleet Street area of London and looked forward to a couple of pints of mild-and-bitter at lunch time. But in the mid-1960s I found that I no longer enjoyed my beer so much. I often had a bad headache or a sour stomach after a few midday pints. I assumed the problem was connected with my own hectic life-style and didn't think to blame the beer.

Then my newspaper moved to a new office just a few yards from a pub owned by a small South London brewery called Youngs. My colleagues suggested I should try a pint of what they called 'real beer'. I followed them cautiously, confusing the name Youngs with Youngers, but I found myself bowled over - literally - by my first few pints of the strong, fruity, tasty ale served with the aid of old-fashioned handpumps. My legs were rather rubbery but I suffered no other after-effects: no headache, no sour gut.

Almost at the same time as I became a regular of the Rose and Crown in Bethnal Green, Richard Boston started to write a weekly column for *The Guardian* on beer, and newspapers reported the activities of a new consumer movement called the Campaign for Real Ale, whose members were dedicated to restoring traditional beer to Britain's pubs. Through Boston and

CAMRA, I discovered that the reason so much beer had a distressing effect on me was not due to a malfunction of my digestive system but because of the way in which modern beer was brewed: filtered, chilled and often pasteurised and then impregnated with excess carbon dioxide gas to give it the kind of fake sparkle in the glass that advertising men believed was necessary to sell their sorry product.

I found, too, that Youngs were not alone in brewing beer that was just the opposite of the big companies' fizzy brands. There were still scores of small regional breweries making beer from natural ingredients and allowing it to ferment and mature in the cask free from brewery processing. Armed with a fast car, a compass, a good map and a list of 'underground' pubs selling the real thing, it was possible to taste the delights of Britain's remaining independent brewers.

The state of British beer and British pubs cannot be divorced from the state of the British brewing industry. As both beer and pubs are vital parts of our way of life, it is reasonable that beer drinkers should know more about the big companies which dominate the industry, and how they have bastardised the liquid in our glasses and many of the places in which we drink. This book sets out to do just that. It is not a history of brewing - there are good books on that subject; neither is it a technical manual on how beer is brewed, though a brief outline is given in the handbook at the end.

It is an attempt to show what has happened to beer and brewing and what consumers can do about the present state of affairs. Above all, it is about the right of consumers to expect quality when they part with their hard-earned money. If it is old-fashioned to talk of quality then I will answer to the charge. But my main concern is not to turn the clock back. It is to look to a future where quality and progress go together, and are not direct opposites, the watchwords of entrenched battalions representing consumers on one side and industry on the other. This book is dedicated as a small contribution to that future.

# 2.

# Big is not beautiful

*'Mergers have inflicted enough damage in the brewing industry; accordingly one hopes the days of mergers are over' — D.M. Wickett, senior lecturer in economics, Sheffield Polytechnic*

Everybody knows there is something seriously wrong with the brewing industry. Drinkers know it, governments know it, the Monopolies Commission knows it. Sadly, little or nothing is done to sort out the mess.

The Monopolies Commission reported in 1969 on the supply of beer. It did not like what it found. Updated to 1977 figures, 50,000 of the country's 66,000 pubs were 'tied houses', that is, owned by brewing companies. And 37,000 of those pubs were owned by the Big Six companies. Whether the landlord of a pub is a tenant, who pays rent to the brewer, or a manager, a salaried employee of the company, he is forced to take the products of the brewery that owns the pub. As the giant combines own more than half the pubs and dominate the club, off-licence, supermarket and 'free' trade, it is clear that they monopolise beer supply, and through that monopoly determine what consumers 'choose' to drink.

The Monopolies Commission concluded that the 'conditions which we have found to prevail operate and may be expected to operate against the public interest since the restrictions on competition involved in the tied house system operated by the brewer suppliers concerned are detrimental to efficiency in brewing, wholesaling and retailing, to the interests of independent suppliers (including potential new entrants), and to

16

the interests of consumers.'

The Commission argued for sweeping changes in the pattern of pub ownership. 'We are of the view that, but for the difficulties of change and transition, a state of affairs in which brewers did not own or control licensed outlets would be preferable to the tied-house system.' It is suggested that 'the licensing system in England and Wales should be substantially relaxed, the general objective being to permit the sale of alcoholic drinks, for on or off consumption, by any retailer whose character and premises satisfy certain minimum standards.'

The Commission had found a situation that was 'against the public interest'. But nothing happened. When the same Commission found some years earlier that the Imperial Tobacco Group had a monopoly position in the production of cigarettes, the London *Evening Standard's* cartoonist Vicky depicted the tobacco combine as a huge white elephant looking round as the Monopolies Commission stuck a pin in its rear. The caption read: 'Stop it, you're hurting.' Change Imperial Tobacco to big brewers and the comment still stands; there is even a close connection between the two industries, for Imperial now own Courage.

The Commission's report on the supply of beer moulders in some special department reserved for forgotten government documents. So does the Erroll Report of 1972, which was asked by the government to look into licensing laws. Erroll echoed the call for an easing of the brewers' grip on the supply of beer by allowing cafes and restaurants to have easier access to licences in the French manner. Erroll's recommendations, which also included more liberal and flexible licensing hours for pubs, joined the Monopolies Commission report in limbo. An attempt to bring some of its provisions into law through a Private Member's Bill in the House of Commons in 1976 failed when a powerful anti-drink lobby of MPs filibustered it into oblivion.

In August 1977, the Price Commission handed down one of the most savage indictments of a major industry ever to come from a government body. In the wake of a series of highly unpopular price increases earlier that year, the Price Commission was asked by the government to investigate brewers' prices and profits. The final result was a wide-ranging survey of the efficiency of major brewers. Four paragraphs of the report's conclusions effectively demolished the long-nurtured myth that the creation of big industrial combines would lead to greater efficiency, profitability and a better deal for consumers:

> 'The large national brewery companies charge higher prices for their beer than regional and small companies. Their prices have increased more rapidly than those charged by regional and small companies.

> 'These above average prices reflect, in large measure, the higher costs of selling, administration and distribution incurred by the large national brewery combines.

> 'Despite the fact that their prices are higher, the large national brewery companies make a significantly smaller net profit margin on their beer than regional and small companies.

> 'The coincidence of higher prices and lower profit margins gives rise to fundamental questions about the trade and its organisation.'

Like the long-forgotten Monopolies Commission report, the Price Commission attacked the tied house system, which, it said, reduced competition and formed an effective barrier to newcomers to the trade. The report found that the big brewers' grip extended far beyond the tied trade: because of their financial muscle they could command a dominating position in the free trade — pubs, clubs and hotels not tied to brewing companies. The report said that in 1976 the Big Six gave loans totalling £115 million to the free trade in return for various forms of a 'partial tie'.

The Price Commission discovered that for all categories of bulk and bottled beer the big brewers charged more than either the regional or the local companies. On average, the big companies charged 2p a pint more than the independents, and between 1974 and 1977 their price increases had been steeper. The trend was most marked for the heavily-promoted lagers: price increases for lager in the same period had averaged 69 per cent for the national companies and 55 per cent for the local firms. The Commission also hinted that the brewers were making an unjustifiable killing from lager: 'The difference in production and marketing costs between lager and a draught beer of the same gravity (strength) is a little over 1p a pint, yet at wholesale prices the difference is some 2p to 3p and at the public house the difference is about 6p. It is obvious therefore that lager is priced on the basis of what the market will stand.'

The brewers had justified every price increase with the claim that their profits were too low and they would not be able to invest in new plant unless they increased their income. The Price Commission was unimpressed and reported that brewing was 'a highly profitable activity' nonetheless. It also shone light on the strange accounting methods of the brewers. About 60 per cent of the brewers' money was tied up in pubs, the report said, yet the companies had no realistic way of measuring how much capital they had invested and could not therefore say what their real profits were. The Commission calculated that the national companies made a 10 per cent profit while the regionals made 13 per cent and the local firms 15 per cent. Turning to brewing and wholesaling, the report estimated that the nationals made a profit of 32 per cent, the regionals 46 per cent and the local firms 53 per cent. The figures were an estimate because the brewers complained that it was 'unrealistic' for them to break down their profits between brewing and wholesaling on the one hand and tied pubs and loans to the free trade on the other.

The Commission made some scathing comments on the nationals' investment programmes, which, according to the brewers, had to be financed through higher prices. They claimed they needed to invest £1,000 million between 1977 and 1980. The Commission said that since the period of major takeovers in the 1960s, the combines had been spending heavily for more than ten years but also asked 'to what degree has the customer benefited from this massive expenditure by the large brewers, most of which, after all, he has paid for in higher prices for his beer? So far as brewing and wholesaling are concerned we have found that large brewers have derived no apparent advantage from larger-scale, more concentrated operations. Their costs and prices are higher and their percentage profit margins lower.'

The current investment programmes, the report went on, were directed in the main at increasing lager production, but the big brewers' past record 'casts serious doubt on whether the planned programme will produce any different result. The brewers argue that they have to raise prices to produce funds for investment and that any restraint on prices would jeopardise the programme. We do not accept as axiomatic that the cost of expansion should necessarily be financed by higher prices. We see a case for a more searching scrutiny of the proposed programme before it is finally undertaken; and certainly before there can be any acceptance of the brewers' claim that the cost should be recouped by putting up the price of beer.'

The report ended with a blunt criticism of the national combines' domination of the industry. The Commission said the combines commanded the industry following the takeovers of the 1960s, and through the chain of control from brewery to pub. The report made no recommendations of how the situation could be remedied but concluded: 'Not only is brewing a highly-concentrated industry but there are significant barriers to entry and virtually no competition from imports. These are the classic conditions for a monopoly which is likely to operate to the detriment of the consumers. The question that has to be asked is whether the present situation is in the public interest or contrary to the public interest. This is the question that must be answered by the government.'

The government has yet to pick up the gauntlet. In fact, it seems to have mistaken the gauntlet for a hot potato and there are fears that Whitehall officials are busily shuffling the 1969 Monopolies Commission report and the 1972 Erroll Report along the shelves to make room for the 1977 Price Commission report. The big brewers were sufficiently stunned by the report to impose a voluntary six-month price freeze, but by January 1978 the lack of any government reaction made them bold enough to seek further price rises. Courage and Scottish and Newcastle were allowed to increase prices by the Price Commission. But when Allied sought a swingeing 3p a pint increase the Commission froze it and ordered an investigation into the group's efficiency, profits and investment programme. It granted Allied an interim increase of 2p a pint.

When the report was first published, the brewers squealed. Through their powerful trade organisation, the Brewers' Society, they complained that the commission just did not understand the difference between running a national brewing combine and running a small regional company, and that different patterns of profit and investment policy applied. The society said that bigger companies had more costly investment in machinery. It made the dubious claim that the Big Six ran better pubs than their small competitors and suggested that the small firms revalued their assets less frequently than the combines. The brewers even hinted at political bias, which was pretty rich coming from an industry that has long been a financial bulwark of the Conservative Party. One apologist for the brewers suggested that the industry was less monopolised than others, and pointed to the bread industry in support. As the bread industry is dominated by three giant national combines and the brewing industry by six, the conclusion to be drawn from that line of argument is that brewing is only half as bad as breadmaking.

But however much the brewers dodged and attempted to hide behind a smokescreen of the government's alleged political animosity, there was no escaping the central and most damaging theme in the Price Commission's findings: that the big brewers' prices were higher and their profits lower than those of the independent companies. It was a picture of incompetence and inefficiency, with the consumers at the receiving end. Throughout the years of takeovers and mergers, the drinkers had been promised, by the newly-emerging combines, 'rationalisation' and 'economies of scale' that would bring cheaper, better and more efficiently brewed beer. The result was just the opposite.

The brewers should not be left to carry all the odium for this singular state of affairs. They are merely part of an industrial system that has for long accepted the axiom 'big is best'; it has led to the creation of vast national and international megacorporations, many of which wield greater financial and political power than national governments. In a study published in 1960, *The Brewing Industry 1886-1951*, Professor John Vaizey's main thesis was that the only viable future for brewing lay in big units of production. He waxed eloquent about the possibilities: the savings to be made from concentrating brewing in a few big centres, the greater efficiency, less waste, the better use of raw materials, and, above all, the better deal the consumers would get. Professor Vaizey predicted that for a brewery to be viable in his vision of the brilliant, super-technocratic, stainless-steel future, it would have to produce a minimum of 50-60,000 bulk barrels a year.

Professor Vaizey proved that if you are going to be wrong you might as well be wrong in a big way. The creation of the national combines has not worked: it has not produced the much-vaunted economies of scale. It is the regional and local breweries, many producing considerably less than 60,000 barrels a year, that are more efficient, successful and profitable - and provide a good service for their customers.

Boddingtons, the Manchester-based independent, is a firm that has stuck firmly to brewing good, traditional beer to suit local tastes. It fought off a sustained takeover bid by Allied Breweries in 1969 and has not suffered as a result. It has refused to expand in all directions and rush its beers to all parts of the country's free trade. CAMRA's paper *What's Brewing* reported in October 1977: 'Boddingtons are the toast of the Stock Exchange this year after topping the *Investors' Chronicle* brewing profits chart. They led a stream of profit successes from small breweries who outstripped all the big national brewers. Boddingtons headed the table of leading profit margins with 19 per cent, ahead of second best Matthew Brown, another firm from the north-west, with 17.7 per cent. The best profit margin figure for a national brewer was 10.3 per cent from Bass Charrington.'

Boddingtons are one of the major independents, brewing 180,000 barrels a year, but the pattern holds good for most of the independent firms that have stuck to their localities and not tried to ape the giants. Another north-west brewer, Jennings of Cockermouth, produces about 24,000 barrels a year and, if Professor Vaizey's analysis had been correct, would have gone bankrupt or been taken over several years ago. But it is trading well in its own quiet way by remaining within its tried and tested trading area. It fought off an attempted takeover by Maxwell Joseph's Mount Charlotte Investments, which wanted to merge

Jennings with the Workington Brewery and close the Cockermouth brewery. Significantly, it is the small firms trying to get big too fast that have run into difficulties: Theakstons of Yorkshire bought a second brewery in Carlisle, expanded at a fast lick into the free trade (its Old Peculier strong ale is now available in most parts of the country) then found it had to raise more money from the bank and take outside investors from the Curwin transport group on to the board.

Why did Professor Vaizey's brave new brewing world fail? The reason is simply that the economies of scale never materialised. Whatever might have happened to processing costs, overall costs increased through the creation of big brewing centres. Before the era of takeovers and mergers, even the comparatively large companies stayed within their own traditional trading areas. They did not run up huge transport and publicity bills. But once they were merged, breweries were closed, local beers were phased out and national processed beers trunked around the country in giant tankers. Between 1966 and 1976 the number of beers brewed in Britain declined from 3,000 to less than 1,500.

Distribution costs soared. So did the cost of promotion. The consumers had to be 'encouraged' to drink the new national beers and vast advertising budgets were drawn up. In the 12 months from September 1976 to 1977, the brewing industry spent £20.34 million on television and press advertising, and an unknown figure on posters. Nearly all of that money was spent by the national combines on their national products. Bass Charrington spent £2.4 million (79 per cent of their total budget of £3.6 million) advertising their lagers, mainly Carling Black Label and Tennents. Whitbread spent £1.5 million promoting Heineken and £450,000 on Trophy bitter. Allied Breweries devoted £620,000 to Double Diamond and £1.7 million to Skol. Guinness were the biggest spenders: £3.1 million was used to promote their bottled and container stouts.

All of these costs are reflected in the selling price of beer. In 1977 publicans in houses owned by the big brewers in the Manchester area complained bitterly that they could not compete with Boddingtons, whose beers were a good 2p to 3p a pint cheaper. In the East Midlands landlords told the Big Six that they were losing trade to pubs owned by the local firms, Hardys and Hansons, Home, and Shipstone, whose excellent beers were pennies cheaper.

The Price Commission found that while the big combines scored over the independents when it came to buying raw materials in bulk, they spent substantially more on production, distribution and selling, which was reflected in profit margins and prices. This is how the wholesale price of a pint broke down in 1976 prices:

|  | Big Six | Regional brewers | Small brewers |
|---|---|---|---|
| Brewing materials, duty and foreign beer purchases | 8.04p | 8.28p | 8.49p |
| Production and packaging | 2.68p | 1.89p | 1.64p |
| Selling, administration and distribution | 3.14p | 2.19p | 1.98p |
| Profit margin | 1.65p | 2.07p | 2.35p |
| Total — wholesale price | 15.51p | 14.43p | 14.46p |

The big brewers must have been glad to see the end of 1977. It was not a good year for them as far as their public image was concerned. Hard on the heels of the Price Commission report came another from ICC Business Ratios, which also concluded that medium and small breweries were far more efficient and cost conscious than the nationals. Writing in the journal of the Brewers' Guild, Stuart Mansell, an experienced City journalist, said that the ICC report was a particularly valuable contribution that went a long way to demolish the brewers' hysterical reaction to the Price Commission report. 'There are many commentators who believe that the major brewers have spent far too heavily - both in terms of capital equipment and promotion - on building up national brews that the average drinker never really wanted in the first place ... The difficulty in pursuing the argument sensibly, however, is that the brewers' case is rarely developed beyond hyperbole. The brewers have persistently declined to back up their arguments with relevant statistics.'

The ICC analysis of profit margin ratios found that Joseph Holt, a small Manchester brewer, came top of the league. The firm's 1975 profit of £583,000 represented 29.7 per cent of sales worth £1.97 million. Next in line came Boddingtons, Oldham Brewery, Matthew Brown and Hardys and Hansons, whose profit margins were around 20 per cent. In contrast, the big brewers had only moderate profits in relation to sales. Scottish and Newcastle had a ratio of 9 per cent, Bass Charrington 8.4, Allied 8.2, Courage 8, Whitbread 6.9 and Guinness 6.8. Mansell commented: 'To all intents and purposes, the big brewers have the narrowest profit margins in the industry, despite charging on average rather more for a pint than their regional competitors. And it does seem valid to conclude, on balance, that this is because they are not running particularly efficient operations.'

Earlier that year the same magazine, *The Brewer*, had published another damaging attack, this time by D.M. Wickett, senior lecturer in economics at Sheffield Polytechnic. He asked what had happened to the planned economies of scale promised by the Big Six. He suggested that as the prices charged by the nationals were usually between 1p and 3p a pint higher than those of the independents, the economies, if they were being achieved, were not being passed on to the customers. 'Does this mean that the economies are simply being taken as higher profits?' Wickett also looked at the profitability of the Big Six by comparing their profits and their assets in conjunction with a random sample of some of the independents. The ratio of profits to assets means that, in the case of Allied, for every £100 invested in plant and equipment, the group makes a profit of £9.06. (See table on page 26.)

Wickett repeated his question: 'So what happened to the economies of scale that the big brewers are supposed to achieve? Could it be that large-scale breweries also have significantly higher transport costs that outweigh the production economies, could it be that they also suffer more labour disputes, offer a less flexible and personal service and in many cases lose custom

25

| The Big Brewers | Profit/Assets (%) |
|---|---|
| Allied | 9.06 |
| Bass Charrington | 7.79 |
| Courage | 5.48 |
| Watney, Mann & Truman | 2.49 |
| Whitbread | 4.63 |
| **The Small Brewers** | |
| J. Arkell | 15.03 |
| George Bateman | 1.45 |
| Boddingtons | 15.00 |
| Eldridge Pope | 9.74 |
| Greene King | 11.59 |
| Higsons | 9.08 |
| Hydes | 13.49 |
| McMullen | 10.53 |
| Morland | 8.46 |
| Timothy Taylor | 16.17 |

because they don't always consider customers' needs?' He quoted a personal survey (the nicest kind of survey where beer is concerned) in South Yorkshire and north Derbyshire in March and April 1977 and produced the following prices for pints of draught bitter:

| | |
|---|---|
| Whitbread Trophy | 28p |
| Stones (Bass Charrington) | 28p |
| Tetley (Allied) | 28p |
| John Smith (Courage) | 27p |
| Wards | 26p |
| Robinson | 26p |
| Home | 25p |
| Hardys & Hansons | 24p |
| Shipstone | 24p |

Wickett was in no doubt that mergers had also restricted the choice for consumers. 'In certain parts of the country some of the big brewers have a very substantial share of a local market and customers may have little or no choice as to whose beer they choose to consume. Local brews are often replaced by national brands and cask-conditioned bitter is often replaced by keg beer.' He quoted the economist Graham Bannock, in his book *The Juggernauts* (1971), who commented on the claim that processed keg beers were provided by the big brewers due to changing demand: 'More probably it simply reflects the exercise of marketing power ... Without tied sales outlets and without heavy selective advertising it is most unlikely that keg beers could have been introduced on anything like the scale so far achieved. As it is, the Juggernaut brewers will soon be in a position to abolish cask beer altogether, although it will no doubt be attributed to the power of the market.'

But before the brewers could manipulate the consumers and change the whole nature of beer, they first had to get big and dominate the market.

# 3.

# A merger has been announced

*'My observation is that these bids are very seldom
beneficial to the customer. For instance, some of the
brews on sale today are little more than sweetened water
and so far as keg beer is concerned, I regard it as a public
fraud.'* — a Boddingtons' shareholder rejecting a
takeover offer from Allied Breweries

Some critics of the modern brewing industry look back to a
golden age when there were no big brewers and magnificent ale
was produced by thousands of small companies. That golden
age never existed. Names such as Bass, Worthington, Courage,
Whitbread and Charrington have been around for more than
two centuries and they have led the rest for a hundred years or
more. Nor are mergers a recent phenomenon. Famous companies such as Ind Coope, Eldridge Pope and Greene King testify to
the fact that small family businesses merged in order to extend
their sales areas and their profitability. Two of the most famous
names in brewing, Bass and Worthington, merged in 1927.

 The difference today is that while there have been major
brewers for some time they did not dominate the industry in the
way today's giant conglomerates do. A hundred years ago, the
big companies were regional companies; with the exception of
Bass, which used canals, rail and sea to transport their beers to
all parts of the country and the empire, they did not attempt to
stray outside their chosen marketing areas.

 A major rationalisation in brewing took place at the turn
of the century. A hundred years ago there were more than 16,000
brewing companies in Britain; today there are 160 operating

breweries owned by 94 companies, individuals, co-operatives and partnerships. Not all of the changes a hundred years ago were for the bad. Many of the pubs were dreadful places selling dreadful beer. As a result many of the smaller brewers went out of business and the bigger companies were quick to snap up their pubs and extend control of the 'tied trade'. The large brewers were helped, too, by their financial power, which enabled them to use more modern methods of brewing, which produced better beer than the murky ale full of slops sometimes served in one-man operated parlours.

The mergers of the 1960s are on a totally different plane. It is no longer a case of hundreds of fish in the pond with a few getting a bit fatter. Now some sharks have infiltrated the pond and swallow everything that gets in their way. They dominate not just beer but other important sectors of the drinks business. The top seven companies, the Big Six plus Guinness, control 89 per cent of the brewing industry.

## 1. Bass Charrington

Bass Charrington are the biggest brewers in Europe. Their origins go back to 1744 when William Worthington started brewing in Burton-upon-Trent. William Bass followed in 1777 and the quality of his beer became a legend. The two firms merged in 1927 but continued to brew their own beers. Bass Worthington entered the league of the giants only in the 1960s when a Canadian called Eddie Taylor came to Britain with a plan to make the country drink the beer that had made him rich and famous back home - Carling Black Label lager.

Within just ten months in 1960 Taylor bought 12 breweries in Scotland and the north. He turned them into a new company, Northern United Breweries, with the addition of four more companies in 1961. Only three of those original 16 firms are operating today and none of their beers has survived. His really big coup came in 1961 when he convinced one of the most famous names in Southern brewing, the family-owned Charrington company, to merge with him to form Charrington United Breweries. In 1963 he added Tennents in Scotland. Taylor paused for three years, then moved into action again. In 1967, after lengthy talks and bargaining, Taylor talked Bass,

Mitchells and Butlers, themselves the result of a merger in 1961, into forming the mighty brewing giant, Bass Charrington. Taylor now controlled 20 per cent of the brewing industry and owned a chain of tied houses throughout the country in which to herd customers into drinking Carling Black Label.

Still Taylor wasn't satisfied. Between 1968 and 1970, Hancocks of Cardiff, Stones of Sheffield and Joules of Staffordshire were stuffed into the Toby jug until, satisfied or satiated, he retired to Canada on the profits of Carling Black Label. At the end of Taylor's brief but momentous visit, he left a vast concern, with breweries throughout the country, 10,000 tied outlets and an annual turnover of £900 million.

Today Bass have 12 operating breweries. Their one new brewery is the enormous Runcorn plant, which, when a £3 million extension is complete, will brew two million pints a day, or more than two million barrels a year, all of it processed beer and lager. Bass have expanded in other directions. They own Britain's third biggest hotel chain, Crest, the soft drinks firm Canada Dry, and a large Belgian brewing company, Lamot. They also have a substantial stake in some independent brewing firms, including Higsons of Liverpool and Maclay of Alloa.

## 2. Allied Breweries

If Bass are the biggest brewers in Europe then Allied are undisputedly the biggest drinks firm. As well as brewing vast quantities of beer, the company also owns Harveys (wines and sherry), Showerings (Babycham), Britvic Fruit Juices, three cider firms, and Teachers whisky. Allied also own 48 hotels and two Dutch brewing companies, Oranjeboom and Breda.

In 1961 three famous names in British brewing, Ind Coope, Ansells and Tetley merged to form the country's second biggest brewers with 15 per cent of the market and 7,600 tied houses. The merger neatly gave the new company a dominant position throughout the country. Ind Coope, which had previously swallowed Allsopp, Benskins, Friary Meux and the Aylesbury Brewing Company, looked after the south, Ansells the midlands and Tetley the north, on both sides of the Pennines. Tetley had merged with Walkers of Warrington in

1960.

In 1969 and 1970 Allied attempted to widen its stake in the industry by taking over the Manchester-based independent, Boddingtons. The West Pennines region was the weakest trading area for the combine and it looked with envy at Boddingtons' success and its 280 pubs. Allied's bid for the firm was worth 3.8 million pounds. Boddingtons' directors dismissed the offer and urged their shareholders to follow suit. A few weeks later Allied increased their offer to £4.5 million. The combine increased the pressure by buying 30 per cent of Boddingtons' shares. Again the independent firm said no. In a letter to shareholders, the chairman, Geoffrey Boddington, said: 'You will be only too aware that present day pressures bear heavily towards the elimination of individuality and character in many consumer goods. There is an inexorable progression towards the mass-produced, nation-wide product of standardised quality. These pressures apply equally to the brewery industry about which it has been said that the standards of tradition set by the independent brewers tend to control the quality of the beers made by the larger groups. If this competition were to cease, if we were left with only five large groups of brewers, British beers would decline to the American standard of cold, chilled and filtered liquids. Instead of the traditional flavours which have made British beer world-famous and unique, the public would be confronted with the limited choice, Brand X, produced under the guise of rationalisation by accountants.'

This rallying cry met with a spirited response from Boddingtons' shareholders. Letters rejecting the Allied offer flooded into the Strangeways brewery in Manchester. They told Allied in decisive terms that their mass produced beers were not wanted in the north-west and that they preferred the regional palate of Boddingtons traditional products. It is unlikely that Allied received such letters from their shareholders when Unilever made a bid for the drinks firm. 'Hands off Double Diamond' is hardly the slogan to stir the nation's beer drinkers.

Allied made one last attempt to buy Boddingtons. In February 1970 the combine increased its bid for Boddingtons' preference shares. Such was the drive to throttle competition in the area and to grab nearly 300 extra tied houses that Allied's bid was now an over-evaluation of the Manchester firm. Boddingtons' bankers advised them to accept the offer but again the company stood firm and advised rejection on the grounds that they had a duty to their shareholders, their customers and their tenants to continue in operation as an independent brewery. Again the shareholders rallied to the company, Allied admitted defeat, withdrew its offer and sold off its shares in Boddingtons.

Boddingtons have had to pay a price for their victory. Whitbread, who have a strong trading position in the north-west, were not keen to see Allied increasing their hold in the region. Whitbread had come to Boddingtons' support by buying shares in the independent. The Whitbread stake today stands at a menacing 26 per cent but Boddingtons' record suggests that the doors of this particular Trojan horse are unlikely to open.

Allied remain determined to improve their trading position in the north-west. At present the combine has seven operating breweries: Ind Coope at Burton and Romford, Ansells in Birmingham, Tetley in Leeds and Warrington and two lager-only plants in Alloa and Wrexham that churn out vast quantities of Skol. In 1977 Allied announced an investment programme to expand production that would cost £164,000,000. Some of that investment will go towards modernising and improving the old Walker brewery at Warrington and the Walker name will be promoted again in a bid to capture some local trade from Boddingtons and the other independent brewers in the region. Allied's programme was praised for its social responsibility by the government and by Jack Jones, then leader of the Transport and General Workers' Union but for a group with assets of £600 million it represents a low level of investment.

## 3. Whitbread

When Whitbread, the oldest of the national brewers, went on the takeover trail, they left behind them a scene of destruction that would make a swarm of locusts envious. In the years between 1960 and 1971, the company closed 15 breweries, 24 bottling plants and scores of distribution centres. By this ruthless campaign, Whitbread transformed themselves from a southern-based company into one of the national giants, with 7,700 tied houses, two soft drinks firms, R. Whites and Rawlings, 1,000 off-licences under the names of Thresher and Stowells, plus Long John International, the whisky firm. Whitbread also own the Onkerzele brewery in Belgium.

When Whitbread started to acquire other companies they set up the 'umbrella' scheme: Whitbread would take a large minority shareholding in a firm that would become an 'associate' company. The end result was often the same as a takeover. While some firms remained associates, most became subsidiaries. Many of the firms lost their identities. They often lost their beers. Sometimes they even lost their breweries.

The first company to come under the umbrella was Andrew Buchan's Rhymney brewery in South Wales. It became part of Whitbread Wales and was closed in April 1978. Others did not survive as long. In 1962, Flowers of Stratford-upon-Avon and Luton became a subsidiary. Flowers was a famous name in Midlands brewing and had the distinction, or otherwise, of being the first company to produce a processed beer with the word 'keg' in the title. Flowers' brand new Stratford brewery was closed and the Luton plant followed when Whitbread built a new, keg-only brewery there in 1969. The City Brewery, Exeter, scuttled under the umbrella in 1962 and was closed in 1967, its activities integrated with those of Starkey, Knight and Ford of Tiverton, Bridgwater and Burnham. Only the Tiverton brewery remains, named Whitbread Flowers.

In 1963 and 1964, Nimmo of Castle Eden and Duttons of Blackburn were taken over and renamed Whitbread East Pennines and West Pennines. In 1965, Lacons of Yarmouth were acquired and promptly shut down. The following year, James Thompson's tied houses in the Barrow-in-Furness area were bought to extend the company's influence in the north-west. In 1967 three breweries belonging to Threlfalls Chesters were bought in Birkenhead, Salford and Liverpool. Birkenhead was closed. In the same year, Campbell, Hope and King of Edinburgh, Evan Evans Bevan of Neath and Isaac Tucker of Gateshead were all bought and shut down. Fremlins of Maidstone and Faversham were more fortunate: only the Maidstone brewery was closed.

In 1972 Brickwoods of Portsmouth became part of Whitbread Wessex. The following year Combined Breweries of Ramsgate were bought and closed, as were Richard Whitaker of Halifax and Bentley of Leeds. West Country Breweries of Cheltenham became Whitbread Flowers and Strong of Romsey in Hampshire tried to find room under the umbrella. Strongs had previously taken over Thomas Wethered of Marlow, Buckinghamshire, and also had a brewery in Newport, Isle of Wight. Newport was closed and Romsey became part of Whitbread Wessex.

When the dust settled, Whitbread emerged with 17 breweries and were well placed in most parts of the country. They had joined the big league but they had left a number of dead and dying around. And almost as an afterthought they had bought a minority share in a number of other brewing companies. They include Boddingtons (26 per cent), Devenish (25), Marston (33), Ruddles (31), Border (20), Brakspear (27), Morland (39) and Buckley (20). All of these companies sell Whitbread products in their outlets and some brew Whitbread beers when the combine is short of capacity. The nagging fear is that Whitbread might at any time increase their stake in one or more of these independents and take them over completely, with the possible loss of their individual beers. Whitbread are heavily committed to lager - they have the British franchise to brew Heineken - and they are building a new £30 million lager-only brewery at Magor in South Wales. The new Samlesbury plant in Lancashire also brews mainly lager, and the firms in which Whitbread have a minority interest could be seen as tempting acquisitions if the company needs extra capacity to brew bitter.

The need for extra brewing capacity could be increased if Whitbread close or sell off some of their older breweries. The closure of Rhymney and Blackburn in 1978 started the alarm bells ringing for several other plants. There are growing fears that Romsey, Wateringbury, Salford, and Castle Eden could be axed in the near future. At first sight it does not seem to make sense for Whitbread to close some of their breweries and then have to make use of other firms' spare capacity. It does make sense, though, if you study Whitbread's role in the property market. In 1976 the company stopped brewing at its famous

Chiswell Street brewery in London, where Whitbread had first started in business in 1742. The site is being redeveloped as office buildings in the heart of the City of London and the American Chase Manhattan Bank are likely to be one of the first tenants. Whitbread will not be taxed on the profits from this development, and might even be able to pay for the new lager plant at Magor out of the tax saved. As Whitbread are advised in their property deals by Trafalgar House, one of the biggest property companies in the country, the fact that there is money to be made from similar brewery closures will not have been lost on the Whitbread moguls. This could mean the end of brewing for some Whitbread plants, and the end of independence for some of the firms in which Whitbread have a sizeable stake.

## 4. Watney Mann and Truman

The creation of the Watney Mann and Truman empire was a long and bloody affair. If he had been a beer drinker, Edward Heath might have seen the 'unpleasant and unacceptable face of capitalism' several years before the Lonrho scandal. The mergers and takeovers that created this modern beer giant killed off some famous names in London brewing. Watney Mann were formed in 1958 by an amalgamation of Watney, Combe Reid, and Mann, Crossman and Paulin. The new company decided to go national quickly. Breweries were bought in Manchester (Wilsons), Northampton (Phipps), Trowbridge (Ushers), Edinburgh (Drybrough) and two in Norwich (Bullards, and Steward and Patteson). The takeovers in Northampton and Norwich were particularly disastrous for drinkers in those areas. The company had an almost total monopoly through its ownership of most of the tied houses, and the two regions began to drown in a sea of fizzy beer.

The new Watney group caught the attention of outside interests anxious to join the 'beerage', as the brewing aristocracy are known. The property man, Charles Clore, tried to buy Watney in 1959 for £21 million. He was rebuffed but Watney were running scared. They decided that the only way to stave off further attempts at takeover was to get bigger. This was the main reason for Watney's takeover of International Distillers and Vintners. The policy did not work. In 1971 the company engaged in a public battle with Maxwell Joseph's Grand Metropolitan leisure empire for another famous London brewing company, Truman, Hanbury and Buxton. Grand Met bid £49 million. It was too high for Watney and they withdrew from the ring. Truman disappeared into the gaping maw of Grand Met. Nevertheless, consumers who did not like Watney's beers (and there were quite a few of them belching around the place) thought that at least the Grand Met takeover of Truman would allow that famous company to continue to brew its own beers, which would not have been the case if Watney had been successful in the battle.

Their joy was shortlived. In 1972 Maxwell Joseph shook the brewing and business world with a mighty £413 million bid for Watney Mann. Concern was expressed that the merging of Watney Mann with Truman would create a brewing monopoly that would effectively wipe out choice for consumers in major parts of the south. Maxwell Joseph put such fears to rest. In April, when he first made his bid, he declared: 'It will be our policy to allow the brewing businesses of Watney and Truman to continue as separate and autonomous units.' As the battle grew hotter, he stressed in May 1972 that 'no rationalisation of the activities of Watney and Truman will take place in the short term and the autonomy of the two companies will be preserved'.

Grand Met's bid was finally successful. At least the two breweries would continue independently, many drinkers in London thought. Such faith in big business was destroyed a year later when Watney Mann & Truman Holdings was set up to form what Grand Met called 'a single profit centre'. It was now firmly part of a giant drinks, hotels and leisure conglomerate, with Watney adding another brewery, Websters of Halifax, and expanding into lager by an arrangement with Carlsberg. As well as beer, wines, spirits, cider and Coca-Cola were produced by the drinks division of Grand Met. Watney's products were available not only in 7,000 tied houses but in Grand Met's catering outlets of Chef and Brewer, Berni Inns and Schooner Inns. From this pinnacle of power, it seemed that Maxwell Joseph could smirk all the way to the bank when a few disgruntled drinkers renamed his brewing subsidiary 'Grotny'.

## 5. Courage

John Courage was founded in 1787 and rapidly became a successful London company. They entered the league of the giants in 1960 with a pincer-like movement that ended in a merger with H & G Simonds of Reading. Courage had earlier merged with Barclay Perkins in 1955 to form Courage and Barclay, but Simonds were no slouches in the takeover game. Between 1919 and 1954 they had taken over some fifteen companies in the south and had 1,500 tied houses. When Courage, Barclay and Simonds were created in 1960 a new and powerful company emerged. It grew more powerful with the acquisition of Plymouth Breweries but it was still too southern-based to be a truly national combine. This weakness was put right through the takeover of John Smith of Tadcaster, which also had breweries in Barnsley and Newark.

The group had 5,800 tied outlets. It looked a tempting bait for a vast combine anxious to expand sales of crisps and cigarettes. In 1972 Courage disappeared into the Imperial Tobacco Group and became just one small cog in a vast machine churning out Golden Wonder Crisps, HP Sauce and hundreds of millions of cigarettes.

A distressing example of how takeovers do not benefit consumers was seen in the case of Barnsley Brewery, a small Yorkshire company famous for the quality of its traditional beer. The brewery was taken over in the early 1960s by John Smith, which announced that they would concentrate their northern activities at Tadcaster. When drinkers of Barnsley Bitter complained, they were told that they would get John Smith's beer in their pubs instead. It did not seem an unreasonable deal, as John Smith also brewed traditional beer.

In 1970 Courage took over John Smith and underscored the decision to close Barnsley and transfer production to Tadcaster. When protests were made to Courage and John Smith by members of the Campaign for Real Ale, who had organised a lively protest march through Barnsley led by local MP Roy Mason, CAMRA were told that the Barnsley Brewery had to close because large sums of money were needed to bring the plant up to date. Parts of the plant had fallen into disrepair and would cost too much to bring into line with safety regulations. Courage claimed that the beer from John Smith would be similar in taste to Barnsley's. CAMRA were not satisfied and asked more questions. Slowly the truth emerged. At Tadcaster, £6,500,000 was being spent to 'modernise' the John Smith brewery. It would produce only 'bright' processed beer served by gas pressure, totally unlike the Barnsley traditional beer. When Courage were asked why it was not possible to divert some of that money to bring Barnsley up to date so that brewing could continue there, the company replied that having two breweries just 28 miles apart was not economic.

If it was not economic, why had first Smith and then Courage bought Barnsley? The answer must be: to close it and kill off competition. Once again the consumers lost out and they are now forced to drink John Smith's bland, pressurised beers in the old Barnsley Brewery pubs.

## 6. Scottish and Newcastle

Many people are surprised to discover that Scottish and Newcastle are one of the Big Six companies. They are not well known outside Scotland and the north-east and they own a mere 1,100 tied houses - such has been the pace of the merger scramble that the word 'mere' can be applied to a company owning more than a thousand outlets for their products. But S & N have a big stake in the free trade and their keg beer, Tartan, is one of the biggest selling national brands.

Scottish and Newcastle were formed in 1960 as the result of a merger between Scottish Brewers and Newcastle Breweries. Although Vaux of Sunderland and Whitbread, Castle Eden offer some competition in the southernmost half of the S & N territory, the merger created a combine that dominated vast stretches of the north-east and Scotland. The financial power given the new company by the merger enabled it to head south and to rival the other national giants through making inroads into the free trade with such processed beers as Tartan and McEwans Export.

Newcastle-upon-Tyne was a city once famous for its range of fine beers. The merger business put an end to that. Newcastle Breweries were formed in 1890 as the result of the amalgamation of several small companies in the area. But there was still a vigorous choice for drinkers as beers came into the area from Scotland and Burton-upon-Trent. Scottish Brewers were created in 1930, merging two famous names in brewing, McEwans and Youngers. Although the two names continued to appear on the company's products, the merger was a portent of the future.

In 1953 the Scottish firm of Robert Deuchar was bought by Newcastle Breweries. James Deuchar, the firm owned by Robert's brother, followed three years later. Both breweries were closed within a few years and Newcastle Breweries had doubled their number of tied houses. In 1959 Newcastle bought up another famous local firm, Rowells, and in 1960 Scottish Brewers acquired Bernards.

In the same year Scottish and Newcastle saw the logic of the pattern the two companies had been following and merged as S & N, with two breweries in Edinburgh and one on the Tyne. They quickly rationalised their activities and the Geordies found that such famous and magnificent brews as Younger's Scotch and McEwan's Special were disappearing from their pubs, to be replaced by the processed beers, Tartan and Newcastle Exhibition. At the same time S & N began to expand their business in the lucrative club trade of the north-east, dominated by the co-operatively run Northern Clubs Federation. The 'Fed' is still king of the clubs in the region but S & N are now major rivals and both produce only processed beers for their clubs.

## 7. Guinness

Arthur Guinness are not one of the Big Six companies because they own no tied houses. But they are a giant brewing concern. Their Dublin brewery is the biggest in Europe and is soon to be enlarged. The company are a major exporter. Although sales of stout are declining in Britain, the beautiful dark beer is becoming popular in Germany and other parts of Europe and there is a great demand for it in Africa. Guinness have a brewery in Nigeria and may expand production there. They are also heavily involved in lager and are major partners in the consortium that own and brew Harp. The other companies are Courage and S & N, with a tiny stake held by Greene King.

urage and S & N are now busy brewing and promoting
own lagers, it seems likely that Guinness will end up
controlling Harp.

Guinness are big because of a unique trading arrangement, going back to before the first world war, which allows their beer to be sold by other brewing companies. Bottled Guinness is available in nearly every pub in the country and the processed container version is fast catching up. Most of the Guinness sold in Britain is brewed in north-west London at the Park Royal Brewery, but some parts of the north-west of England are lucky enough to get the superior Irish Guinness.

By the mid-1970s the big brewers had consolidated their grip on the beer industry. A study of the growth of their profits is one way to measure the extent of their domination. In 1972 and 1977 the pre-tax profits of the Big Six were:

|                      | 1972  | 1977   |
|----------------------|-------|--------|
| Bass Charrington     | £49m  | £90m   |
| Allied               | £54m  | £77m   |
| Watney               | £30m  | £40m*  |
| Whitbread            | £21m  | £42m   |
| Scottish & Newcastle | £20m  | £31m   |
| Courage              | £15m  | £33m   |

*Does not include profits from managerial houses which come under Berni Inns.

1977 was a comparatively poor year for the brewers as a result of the wet summer. Their profits had been record ones in the heatwave years of 1975 and 1976. Their profits have grown by more than 13 per cent year by year over the period. They may be smaller as a percentage of total assets than those of the independent companies but they remain big nevertheless, and they are not fully used for investment. For example, in the two years 1976 and 1977, Bass Charrington had £182 million available for investment, but invested only £103 million in fixed assets, Allied had £171 million available but invested only £105 million, Scottish and Newcastle invested £36 million out of £77 million, Whitbread £55 million out of £113 million, and Courage £37 million out of £80 million (1975 and 1976).

By 1977 the market share of the top seven companies was: Bass 20 per cent; Allied 16 per cent; Watney 14 per cent; Whitbread 12 per cent; S & N 10 per cent; Guinness 9 per cent (including Harp lager); and Courage 8 per cent. In other words, the top seven firms control 89 per cent of the brewing and distribution of beer, leaving some 87 other brewing concerns to share the remaining 11 per cent of the market. Nine out of ten pints of the 32 million consumed every day in Britain are brewed by the national combines. While many of the smaller regional and local firms are flourishing as a result of the revival of traditional beer, their production figures scarcely show on the national graph. Ruddles of Oakham in Leicestershire doubled their production in 1976 and they are now brewing 100,000 barrels a year. That is small beer compared to the two million barrels a year from just one Bass brewery at Runcorn. Jennings of Cockermouth's annual production represents 0.13 per cent of British beer; if they doubled their production they would still produce only a quarter of one per cent of the country's beer.

The takeover battles are by no means over. In 1969 Allied Breweries had to fight off a bid by Unilever and, given the right political climate, a similar bid might be made again. In 1972 Northern Foods bought up the Hull Brewery and then bought a substantial stake in Tolly Cobbold of Ipswich, itself the result of an earlier merger between Tollemache and Cobbold. Bass Charrington were not happy with the ambitions of Northern Foods. They had also bought shares in Tolly and put their own man on the board as chairman. The Ipswich company also used its spare capacity to brew beer for Bass's East Anglian outlets. Bass's interest in Tolly was a holding operation. Nervous of impending government reports on the industry, they did not want to take over Tolly outright but they were determined to baulk Northern Foods until a better prospect came along. It arrived in the shape of a shipping firm, Ellerman Lines, which had taken over the Hartlepool brewers, Camerons, in 1975 for £14 million. In August 1977 Ellerman made a surprise and ful bid for Tolly worth £5.7 million.

Both Camerons and Tolly continue to trade under their familiar names but Ellermans are firmly in control and are now the ninth biggest brewing group in Britain, with 1,110 tied houses. Why did Bass stop Northern Foods and allow Ellermans to grab Tolly? Is it because the shipping firm is not a major threat to Bass while an expanding Northern Foods could begin to challenge the hegemony of the other big drinks and food combines? Pub for pub, Ellerman's bid for Tolly was much lower than for Camerons, which shows just how eager Tolly's board were to escape the clutches of Northern Foods and to get the guarantees they wanted on the Ipswich brewery.

In January 1978 there were rumours of an impending bid for the small Birmingham brewers, Davenport, while Whitbread were thought to be contemplating the takeover of Morland of Abingdon. The takeover trail is not yet ended.

# 4.

# Beer, beer everywhere, nor any drop to drink

*'We believe we have a good social conscience' — a Watney executive on his company's attitude to rural pubs*

The Big Six combines emerged from the takeover scramble of the 1960s owning 37,000 tied public houses, more than half of the country's pubs. That is a lot of pubs, and the figure is distorted by the fact that few bars in Scotland and Northern Ireland are tied to breweries. In those regions the tradition is for bars to be free, though the severe lack of choice means they have little option but to take beer from the giants. In the whole of the UK there are 22,900 free houses, mainly pubs but including clubs and hotels. Many of them are free only in name and are forced by the lack of choice in their areas or by financial inducements to sell beer brewed by the nationals.

The ownership of tied houses gave the combines the coverage to serve their beers to the public in all parts of the country. The pattern of ownership that emerged at the end of the merger period gave most of the big brewers such dominance in some areas that choice was virtually wiped out: either you drank the beer of the monopoly dominating your area or you went thirsty.

Three of the giants in particular had built themselves impregnable positions in four large regions: Watney in Norfolk and Northamptonshire, Courage in Avon and Ind Coope (Allied Breweries' southern arm) in the mid-Chilterns area of Buckinghamshire and Hertfordshire. The situation is not much better in other parts: in Birmingham, for example, the Bass subsidiary Mitchells and Butlers, and Allied's Ansells, hold sway, while large parts of the north-east and Scotland are no-man's land for all but Scottish and Newcastle, and Tennents.

Norfolk is an especially grim example of what happens when one company rules supreme. The county has no independent breweries and has been designated a 'beer desert' by the Campaign for Real Ale. The remaining brewers in Norfolk disappeared when Watney swallowed Bullards, and Steward and Patteson in Norwich, and Whitbread bought and closed Lacons in Great Yarmouth. Now Watney own 70 per cent of the tied houses in Norfolk and all of them get the same processed beers from its Norwich brewery. Just 134 pubs in the entire county belong to other brewers. According to a report produced by CAMRA's Monopolies Committee in November 1977, in 12 of the 13 licensing areas of Norfolk, Watney have an average of 64 per cent of full licences. In Norwich they have 65 per cent, in spite of the fact that they swapped 40 pubs with Courage for houses in Avon in 1972. Under current anti-monopoly legislation, ownership of 25 per cent of tied houses is sufficient to establish a monopoly. But before official action can be taken you have to prove that the monopoly is being abused.

Thetford in Norfolk is the birthplace of Tom Paine, author of *The Rights of Man*, who helped inspire the French and American revolutions. There is a pub in Thetford called the Rights of Man but it is unlikely to be the launching pad of an insurrectionary movement in the county, for it is a Watney's pub. This is a calumny on a man who believed in and fought for freedom, but the pub is certainly not alone in being fettered to a giant: 13 of the 16 pubs in Thetford are owned by Watney.

Thetford's magistrates court keeps the licensing statistics for five of Norfolk's 13 licensing districts. The file on the East Dereham district shows that Watney own the licences for 48 of the 56 pubs. There are no other tied houses in an area measuring more than 20 miles in diameter. The districts of Thetford, Wymondham, Diss, East Dereham and Swaffham cover half the county and in that region Watney own 169 pubs. Whitbread have 17, Greene King three and Adnams and Bass one each. There are 36 free houses but many of them are not really free at all: they depend on Watney for their supplies.

Norfolk is mainly a rural area and pubs are traditionally

the centre of village life. Watney went on a rampage when they first arrived in the region, closing down scores of village pubs. More than a quarter of their pubs in the five districts controlled by Thetford have been closed since 1963. In that year there were 296 pubs, of which Watney owned 229. In 1977 there were 227 and Watney owned 169. In the Wymondham district 90 per cent of the villages with only one pub are under the sway of Watney.

At least those villages still have one pub each, even if the residents are not jumping for joy about the beer on sale in them. Many villages in Norfolk are now 'dry'. The inhabitants have to go to the next village or beyond for a drink and a social get-together. The journeys are difficult because bus services are poor or non-existent. It is hazardous to go by car because of the police and the breathalyser, and when you do get to the next village the odds are that the beer on offer will be Watney's. In one licensing district served by Downham Market on the edge of the Fens, Watney have closed 27 pubs in the past 11 years and crippled the social life of the area in the process. There are only 22 Watney pubs left and nine owned by other companies or free of the tie. Among 16 towns and villages in the district, three have been left publess by closures since 1966 and for most others the word choice has become a joke.

The village of Stiffkey in northern Norfolk has two claims to fame. In the 1920s its vicar was publicly defrocked by the local bishop for improper behaviour; he ended his life as a circus stuntman when he was mauled to death by a lion. In modern times Stiffkey has achieved an ever sadder fame as the village that Watney killed. It has a population of 400 and once boasted three pubs, supplied by Bullards, and Steward and Patteson. Then Watney bought the breweries. In 1966 the company closed the Victoria in Stiffkey and three years later the Red Lion was shut. The villagers had no choice but to crowd into the Townshend Arms and sup the Watney's beer, but even that small pleasure was denied them in 1971 when Watney put the pub up for sale. Nobody in the village could raise the money and the pub was closed. The tragedy of Stiffkey was first told in Christopher Hutt's savage polemic *The Death of the English Pub*. Alan Tuck, the village's retired postman, remembers when Stiffkey was a thriving village: 'The death of the Townshend

Arms was the final straw. Since then the post office and last shop have closed and with the last pub went the thriving cricket team. No teams would come to play us once the pub had shut. It was just about the last meeting place left in the village.'* Now the villagers, most of whom have no cars, have to go three miles to Wells-Next-The-Sea for a drink. It is a long walk as there is no bus service.

A distressingly similar situation exists in Northampton-shire, where again Watney rule supreme. The company own almost 55 per cent of the pubs in the county and the figure is more than 70 per cent in the mid-Northants licensing area. In the county town, 68 per cent of the pubs are owned by Watney. When CAMRA's Monopolies Committee surveyed the county in 1977 it found that 'the monopoly has enabled the brewer to determine his system of production and dispense with no reference to the consumer and without this power total conver-sion [to processed beer] would not have taken place.' Watney have introduced a new beer into the region on a test market. It is a traditional draught beer and does bring some relief for the victims of Watney's fizz but the CAMRA report said: 'Watney's Fined Bitter is priced at up to 5p a pint more than local prices for similar gravity beer from other brewers, which might be considered an exploitation of the monopoly.'

In Avon in 1977 Courage owned 535 of the county's 952 full on-licences. When CAMRA's Monopolies Committee studied the county it found that Courage's control had been used to phase out a lot of traditional beer in favour of the processed variety. 'In Bath, where Courage own 48 per cent of pubs, traditionally-dispensed beers are retained in 65 per cent of the pubs. But in Bristol, where Courage own 69 per cent of the pubs, less than a third sell traditional beer. The Courage brewing operation in Bristol is on a large scale by brewing standards and enjoys a high volume but compact distribution area. If any advantages are derived from this situation, which would be expected, we can see no evidence to indicate that the resulting advantages are benefiting the customer either through price,

*'Ale-less in Watney land' by C. Hutt and F. Pearce in *What's Brewing*, August 1977.

variety or quality.' The report concluded: 'In Avon, Courage's monopolistic power is used to control and manipulate market activity against the interest of the consumer.'

In the mid-Chilterns area, Ind Coope owned 475 of the 683 pubs in 1977. That is 69.5 per cent, far in excess of the 25 per cent laid down in the anti-monopoly laws. I visited two towns in the area, Berkhamsted in Hertfordshire and Chesham in Buckinghamshire, to sample pub life under the paternalistic regime of Ind Coope. Some of the pubs in these towns bore witness to the fact that they are owned by the Aylesbury Brewery Company, but this firm has not brewed beer since 1937 and since 1972 has been a subsidiary of first Ind Coope and Allsopp and now Allied Breweries. Just walking up the high street of Berkhamsted and round by its canal, I counted 14 pubs owned by Ind Coope or its subsidiary: the Swan, the Crown, the Bull, Black Horse, Goat, Brownlow Arms, George, Lamb, Carpenters Arms, Rose and Crown, Crooked Billet, Crystal Palace, Boat and Rising Sun. Those who are allergic to Ind Coope beers may try walking up the road to the village of Northchurch, which is really just an extension of the town - but they won't find much relief. Northchurch has two pubs, the George and Dragon and the Old Grey Mare. Both are owned by Ind Coope.

Chesham is a bigger town but it is scarcely any better off for beer. I passed just some of its pubs - the Jolly Sportsman, the Waggon and Horses, the Cock, George and Dragon, Queen's Head, King's Arms, Red Lion and Golden Ball - all of them tied to Ind Coope. I was told there was one Courage pub in the town but I couldn't find it and retired to the Queen's Head which Ind Coope have mercifully allowed to sell Brakspear's splendid beers.

Norfolk, Northamptonshire, Avon and the mid-Chilterns have all been referred by CAMRA to the Office of Fair Trading with a request that the office should ask the Monopolies Commission to take action against the companies concerned, which are clearly in breach of the monopolies laws. It was probably the fear of action that led Courage, Allied and Bass to announce in September 1977 that they intended to swap 437 pubs between them, in areas where they each have an existing monopoly of the tied estate. By early 1978 Courage gave up 73 pubs in Bristol, 45 of them going to Allied and 28 to Bass Charrington. Courage lost a further 72 pubs in the Thames Valley, 45 to Bass and the rest to Allied. On this basis, Courage gained 85 pubs in the west midlands; Allied's Ansells subsidiary lost 32 to Courage and Bass's Mitchells and Butlers gave 12 to Allied and the rest to Courage. Allied gave up 43 pubs in the mid-Chilterns (29 to Courage and 14 to Bass) and on Merseyside 20 pubs switched from Allied's Tetley to the John Smith's offshoot of Courage. There was some minor tinkering in a few other areas.

The companies concerned maintain their monopolies. For example, Courage still own 58 per cent of the pubs in Bristol and 55 per cent in the county of Avon. The consumers are no better off. In some areas they are worse off, for like has not been swapped with like. In Liverpool, several of the Tetley pubs which were exchanged with John Smith sold traditional beer, while John Smith produce only processed beer. It is likely that the new Courage pubs in the West Midlands will be served only with processed beers when the company's new multi-million keg-only brewery opens at Worton Grange near Reading, or from their subsidiary, John Smith's plant at Newark. And whether the beers are traditional or processed, they will be different in strength and palate to the beers they have replaced.

The brewers may have shuffled a few places on the Monopoly board, but the drinkers, as always, have not been consulted. They will still get the beer the combines want them to drink, which is not at all the same thing as the beer they would like to drink.

# 5.

## Today East Sheen, tomorrow the world...

> '*The extra outlets resulting from mergers and larger areas also required the customers to be persuaded to accept national products, recognisably different from the traditional ales and this factor increased the role of marketing and advertising*' — *John Marks, writing in* Lloyds Bank Review, *1974*

Once the Big Six controlled most of the market and the tied outlets, they set about the task of changing the entire nature of British beer. Processed beers existed before the big monopolies were created but it needed their stranglehold on the industry to allow such beers to expand their market at a fast rate and to replace and almost kill off traditional beer.

In the brewing industry, traditional draught beer and processed beer are known respectively as 'cask-conditioned beer' and 'brewery-conditioned beer'. They are rather a mouthful, and CAMRA coined the phrase 'real ale' as a useful way to describe traditional beer. Processed beer is known as 'keg' because that is the name given to the special pressurised containers used to store the beer. Brewers do not like the expression real ale and angrily claim that all their beer is real - which shows that belief in life after death is not just confined to the godly. The fact is, traditional beer continues to ferment and mature in the cask after it has left the brewery while keg beer is quite dead and is chilled, filtered and often pasteurised before reaching the pub. Like other natural foods, traditional beer has a short life. Because it is open to the atmosphere for up to 48 hours in the pub cellar before it is ready to serve, its quality

49

slowly deteriorates. It will be in good condition for about a week and will then become sour and undrinkable. Care is needed to keep the beer in good condition, to make sure the cellar temperature is neither too hot nor too cold and to ward off anyone who might wander into the cellar and give the casks a good kick, which would stir up the sediment and produce a murky pint.

Processed beer started almost by accident. In 1936 the East Sheen Tennis Club in the Surrey commuter belt complained to Watney that they were having trouble with their beer. The club didn't sell much during the week and the beer was often in poor condition by the weekend. Some of their members refused to drink it and there was a lot of expensive wastage as a result. By sheer coincidence, Watney were experimenting with a new type of beer at the time. The beer was pasteurised in the brewery to stabilise it, and was then placed in a sealed container impregnated with carbon dioxide gas. It was a sterile beer that would last for several months, or have a 'long shelf life' in brewers' parlance. As the beer was dead, further carbon dioxide would need to be applied to serve the beer, and the sealed cannisters or kegs, as they became known, were supplied complete with cylinders of $CO_2$. This experimental beer was meant for troops in India, but Watney diverted some to the less remote part of the empire in East Sheen. The beer was called Watney's Red Barrel and it was to revolutionise the beer industry.

Brewers have always been concerned, and rightly so, with the problems created by traditional, cask-conditioned beer. Only an impossible romantic would dismiss these problems. Certainly, in the days before keg came to dominate the market, an awful lot of sour and cloudy beer was served up in pubs throughout the country and the filthy habit of pouring the slops back into the cask was widespread. Brewers of quality beer were also concerned that, even with devoted landlords and cellarmen who looked after the beer and kept their pipes and pumps scrupulously clean, something could happen - perhaps a sudden spell of hot, muggy weather - that would result in a bad pint.

The trouble was that the big brewing companies drew all the wrong conclusions: wrong, that is, for the consumers but right as far as their accountants and profits graphs were concerned. Instead of relentlessly pursuing quality, training bar staff and ensuring that pub cellars and their serving equipment were always in top condition, the brewers plumped instead for processed, sterile beer that required not devoted cellar work but the ability to handle a spanner in order to connect the keg to its gas cylinder.

Small amounts of keg beer were produced in the 1940s and 1950s, but the production was mainly for clubs and remote pubs with a slow turnover. It needed the arrival of the national combines to transform keg from an insignificant beer to market leader. The new conglomerates were concerned with profit rather than quality. Of course, all brewing companies are in business to make money but it is fair to say that of the independent companies I have visited, quality of product is always the watchword, while in the big, modern stainless steel megakeggeries of the brewing giants, maximising production in order to maximise profit is the guiding principle.

In 1959, keg beer accounted for just 1 per cent of beer sales. By 1965 it was 7 per cent, by 1971, 18 per cent. The fizzy juggernauts rolled on and by 1976 brewery-conditioned beer in kegs and tanks represented 63 per cent of beer production. More than 20 per cent of that figure was accounted for by lager, which hardly existed before the national takeover scramble. In the same year, traditional beer represented 14 per cent of sales, with 23 per cent accounted for by canned and bottled beer. Within 16 years the industry had been stood on its head and what had been the norm, traditional draught beer, was now a sideline for the big brewers, who looked on its production as an irritating diversion from a new 'norm'. Watney, Mann and Truman were sufficiently irritated by it to decide on phasing out all production of cask-conditioned beer. Of course, nobody bothered to ask the drinkers whether they preferred processed beers. They were simply forced to drink them, because within a few years three-quarters of the pubs in Britain offered only keg beer. The brewers then claimed there was a 'growing demand' for this kind of beer, though there are no reported demonstrations in the early 1960s by drinkers chanting 'we want keg' outside the major brewing companies.

Not only had the brewing companies changed; the men

who ran them had changed, too. Devoted craftsmen led by skilled brewers were replaced by technicians, scientists and accountants who were remote from their customers, their publicans and even their beer.

Profit ruled. And the way to make the profits even bigger was to exploit the advantages of having thousands of tied houses in every part of the country. Now the big companies wanted national beers, heavily promoted, with a good brand image, that could be trunked to every pub within the chain. It was a policy that spelt death for thousands of local, traditional beers brewed to meet local, traditional tastes.

It has already been seen that between 1966 and 1976, the number of beers dropped from 3,000 to less than 1,500. This massacre brought no joy to the consumers. When Watney took over Tamplins of Brighton and Henty and Constable of Chichester in 1953 and 1954, they replaced the two distinctive beers brewed by the firms with one new beer called Sussex Bitter. Complaining customers were mollified by the fact that at least Sussex Bitter was preferable to the national Watney beers, Red, Special and Starlight. But Sussex Bitter was withdrawn in 1970 and replaced by Watney's Special. A spokesman for Watney explained: 'We are sorry to see Sussex Bitter go but tastes change. The decision to discontinue this beer has not been taken lightly but its sales have not been buoyant and have lately been falling steadily; at the same time, sales of Watney's Special Bitter have been growing fast throughout the south of England.'

Of course they had, because newspaper readers and television viewers were being bombarded daily with clever advertisements urging them to drink Watney's Special. The demise of Sussex Bitter was aided by the fact that Watney representatives had for some months encouraged landlords in the area to take Special instead, and the company had even refused to send supplies of Sussex Bitter to some pubs. Demand for a beer does tend to decline if you cannot find it anywhere.

A similar pattern followed in other areas. When Watney swallowed Bullards, and Steward and Patteson in Norfolk, their beers were discontinued and replaced by one beer, Norwich Bitter. When Bass Charrington brought in a new beer, Brew Ten, in the north of England, landlords were told that they could

52

no longer have supplies of Stones Bitter from Sheffield, a Bass subsidiary. A spokesman commented, in the style of George Orwell's Newspeak: 'It is not true that Stones is being discontinued, merely that Brew Ten is being promoted.'

The process is by no means finished. When Courage's vast new brewery at Worton Grange is completed it will replace the old Simond's brewery in Reading that produces excellent draught beer as well as the processed variety. But Worton Grange, dubbed a 'fizz factory' by CAMRA, will produce only keg bitter and lager. Production of the cask beers will be switched to other Courage breweries in the south and will be trunked up to the Reading area. But it is unlikely that the other breweries will be able to match the subtle tastes of the former Reading brews, and local Berkshire palates may rebel against them. Perhaps demand will fall. Never mind, Worton Grange will be pumping out millions of gallons of heavily-promoted keg beers. There will be beer for Berkshire even if it is not the beer that Berkshire would like.

With the introduction of keg beer the consumers lost out all along the line. They lost their local beers and often their local breweries. They were forced to drink nationally promoted processed beers that tasted quite different and they had to pay more for them as the cost of promotion, conditioning and distribution was added to the price in the pub. A survey by *Which?* magazine in 1972 showed that when a keg beer was compared with a cask beer from all the major combines, the kegs were usually 2p a pint more although the cask beer was stronger than the keg in most cases. The situation has not improved since that survey was carried out. As we shall see when we turn to lager, high prices and low strength are a growing problem.

The type of beers and their promotion went hand in hand. To utilise their tied properties effectively, the brewing combines developed a handful of national brands that would be recognisable everywhere: Allied's Double Diamond, Courage's Tavern, Bass Charrington's Worthington E, Younger's Tartan, Watney's Red and Whitbread's Tankard. These beers underwent a complete brewery conditioning so that they were dead when they were put into their sealed containers, with the remaining space filled by carbon dioxide gas. Some keg beers are so heavily gassed that they act like an aerosol: when the keg is connected up for service, the gas pressure forces the beer out and up to the bar. Other beers that are not so heavily impregnated with $CO_2$ still have gas cylinders connected to the kegs to force the beer to the bar from the cellar. The beers are also chilled to help mask their lack of flavour. Flavour can only develop in a beer if it is allowed to undergo a natural secondary fermentation in the cask.

A row over carbon dioxide has spluttered on over the years. Supporters of traditional beer argue that $CO_2$ does considerable harm to beer. The brewers of keg beer disagree and point to the fact that $CO_2$ is given off naturally by beer in the course of its production. That is true, but it misses the point. With a cask of traditional beer, most of the natural $CO_2$ will escape when the cask is tapped prior to serving the beer. $CO_2$ cannot escape from a sealed keg, and dissolves into the beer. Brewers also argue that the gas is tasteless and odourless. Equally true, but when carbon dioxide is dissolved in beer it forms carbonic acid, which has a sharp, acidic flavour. It is this dissolved $CO_2$ that gives keg beer its gassy 'bite', which can lead to headaches and sour stomachs. Whitbread actually promote Tankard as 'the bitter with bite'.

The traditional local beers replaced by the national keg brands had a wide and infinite variety of tastes: bitter beers, sweet beers, hoppy beers and malty beers. As there was no way in which one national brand could replace such a wide range of beers, the brewers deliberately designed the new beers to be bland, without sharp and definite tastes. The blandness might not excite drinkers but neither was it likely to upset them. Drinkers used to a bitter, hoppy beer would not complain that their new national keg was too malty and vice versa. When the long-running Watney's Red Barrel was replaced by a new keg beer in 1971 called simply Red, a press statement said the new beer had a 'blander taste, a better head and less unpleasant after effects', the last phrase presumably being a reference to the fact that as it was extremely weak it was hard to get drunk on it. The reference to a better head is also revealing. It is part of the marketing people's ideology that the look of a product is as important, if not more important, than its taste and quality. One reason for this, where beers like Watney's Red are concerned, was to woo the younger generation of the 'swinging sixties' and it was thought that bright, light-coloured, frothy near-beer full of zesty gas bubbles would help to win them from Coca-Cola and Seven-Up. When a *Sunday Times* journalist asked one of the brewers of Harp lager in 1974 to explain its success the brewer replied: 'It's not so much what you can say for it. It's just that there's not much you can say against it.' Commenting on the *Sunday Times* article, Frank Baillie, one of the most knowledgeable writers on beer, said in *What's Brewing*: 'Harp was a marketing man's beer if ever there was one. Harp was described as the most modern of modern beers, a beer which isn't a beer, in which clarity replaces body, fizz replaces flatness and a sparkling golden colour rounds off the presentation to fit the marketeers' great discovery - that not so many people liked beer as liked the idea of it.'

The advertising and marketing departments of the big brewers overcame the problem that there was not much to be said in favour of their new beers. The 'demand' had to be created by a massive arm-twisting exercise. In 1977, as we have seen, more than £20 million was spent on advertising beer and almost all of that was devoted to keg beers and lagers. The big brewers claim - though they have been forced to change their tune a little of late - that there is no demand for traditional draught beer. It is hardly surprising when they spend virtually no money promoting it. You cannot expect people to ask for something that they assume does not exist. With the exception of bottled Guinness, which is a naturally-conditioned beer allowed to mature in the bottle, the brewing combines spend very little on advertising or promoting traditional beer, save for drip mats in pubs and small window stickers saying 'traditional beer sold here'.

An interesting example of the logic of the beer giants can be seen in the way Bass Charrington promote two of their most famous beers, the keg Worthington E and the cask-conditioned draught Bass. Worthington E has been heavily advertised on television in a series of clever commercials that conjure up memories of the first world war and the 1920s as happy E swillers burst into song and toast young ladies called Daisy and

Sally before wishing us all goodbye-eee. Meticulous care is taken to get the period feeling of the commercials. One luckless actor hired to play a soldier in a Great War commercial was given his marching orders when it was discovered just before the cameras rolled that Tommies of the time weren't allowed to wear beards. The advertising agency behind the commercials drove some 3,500 miles around the country in search of just the right rural pub for the Daisy, Daisy plug, in which our heroine arrives with her gentleman friends on a tandem to partake of the sparkling beverage.

The object was to boost Worthington E with an appeal to sentimentality and tradition. This is good old beer, runs the message, enjoyed by your grandparents and parents and still available in thousands of pubs today. In fact, it is nothing of the sort. The Worthington E enjoyed by the Daisies, Sallies and Tommies of yesteryear was a natural beer, conditioned in the cask, while the modern version is a fully-fledged keg, chilled, filtered, pasteurised - and killed - in the brewery.

I suggested to one of Bass Charrington's top publicity men, Jim Lloyd, that the commercials might confuse the public and make them think that Worthington E was still a traditional beer. He did not agree: 'We just have a different attitude to you as to what traditional beer is,' he said. But why choose E when you could choose draught Bass, just as old and truly traditional? 'Simply,' said Mr Lloyd coolly, 'because we sell four times as much E as Bass.'

That is not surprising. According to the Media Expenditure Analysis for 1977, Bass Charrington spent £310,000 on promoting Worthington E on television and in the press. The analysis does not mention a single penny being spent on draught Bass. In fact, some money is spent. Posters in the north-west, in Bass pubs, urged drinkers to 'ask for cask', which includes draught Bass, and a small leaflet extolling the virtues of the ale has been distributed. Bass is described as 'one of the great ales of old England' but not so great that it can feature in any press or television advertising.

The incessant promotion of the national keg brands paid handsome dividends for the brewers. By 1972 the *Financial Times* estimated that the profit margin on kegs and lager was approximately 50 per cent more than on draught beer. Since then, the even heavier promotion of the weak but expensive lager will have increased that margin.

Another simple way to make more profit is to brew weaker beer. There is the famous 1930s depression song:

> I'm the man, the very fat man,
> That waters the workers' beer.
> Yes, I'm the man, the very fat man,
> That waters the workers' beer.
> What do I care if it makes them ill,
> If it makes them horribly queer -
> I've a car, a yacht, and an aeroplane,
> And I waters the workers' beer.

Of course, that is a thing of the past, of the bad old days. Or is it? The fact is that beer has been getting weaker throughout this century but it has not been getting noticeably cheaper. Compared with other consumer prices, the price of beer has remained fairly constant, but its strength has not. The Customs and Excise Department levy duty on beer according to its strength, known as its 'original gravity' or OG for short. This measurement is taken at the start of the fermentation process and is based on the amount of fermentable material - malted barley, sugar and hops - added to the water, which has a gravity of 1000 degrees. A beer with a gravity of 1036 degrees has had 36 parts of fermentable material added to the water. In 1976, the standard rate of duty on a 36 gallon barrel of beer was £15.84 plus VAT. On top of that standard rate, extra duty was added for each degree of gravity above 1030 at a rate of 58.2p per degree plus VAT. You do not have to be a mathematician to see that if a brewer producing millions of gallons of a certain brand each year drops the gravity by one degree and maintains or even increases the price of beer, then he will make a killing.

When Christopher Hutt looked at this subject in the early 1970s he found that Watney's Special Bitter had fallen in gravity from 1043.1 in 1960 to 1037.9 in 1971. Based on the excise duty rates of 1971, he estimated that each barrel of Watney's Special brewed at its 1971 gravity was costing the company £2.64 per barrel less in excise duty than if its strength had been maintained. A year later, the OG of Watney's Special had fallen to 1036, a further saving of 44 pence a barrel.

In 1960 Worthington E had an OG of 1041.8. In 1971 the OG had fallen to 1036.8. In the same period Ansell's bitter in the midlands had fallen in gravity from 1045.3 to 1038.9. The *Sunday Mirror* started to wage war with the brewers in the early 1970s on the strength - or lack of it - of their beers. In 1971 the paper declared that Ind Coope's Superdraught, Whitbread Starbright, Ansells' Kingpin Keg, Watney's Starlight and Watney's Special Mild were all so weak that they would have been legal during American prohibition. The *Sunday Mirror* said of one of these brews: 'Watney's Special Mild, apart from having the least alcohol in it, also propped up the pile with an OG rating of 1030.4. This brew is so weak that if it dropped in strength by about 1 per cent alcohol it would be classed as "near beer" and could be sold to children as mineral water.'

The brewers were considerably embarrassed by this adverse publicity. Most of the miserable brews mentioned by the *Sunday Mirror* disappeared from the market (or were re-labelled and sold to children as mineral water) and within a couple of years the OG of Worthington E had crept up to 1039.1 and was the strongest of the national keg brands. When CAMRA's newspaper *What's Brewing* tested the OGs of all the national kegs it came up with the following list:

| | |
|---|---|
| Double Diamond (Allied) | 1037.8 OG (3.5% alcohol) |
| Worthington E (Bass) | 1039.1 OG (4.2% alcohol) |
| Tavern (Courage) | 1038.0 OG (3.8% alcohol) |
| Tartan (S & N) | 1035.9 OG (3.9% alcohol) |
| Watney's Red | 1037.8 OG (3.4% alcohol) |
| Tankard (Whitbread) | 1038.5 OG (3.9% alcohol) |

An important breakthrough for the consumer came in 1976 when the *Good Beer Guide* published a list of the original gravities of all traditional draught beers brewed in

Britain. They showed that the beers produced by the independent brewers were, on the whole, stronger and considerably cheaper than those of the national combines. The following year, the Food Standards Committee of the Ministry of Agriculture reported on the composition and labelling of beer and recommended that some indication of the strength of beer should be given at the dispensing point in the pub. They suggested that an X rating system should be introduced, from one X for low gravity beer to five for strong beers of the barley wine type.

As a result of all this activity on the gravity front, the average strength of beer has started to increase slightly. In 1968 the average OG was 1037.36; in 1971 it had fallen to 1036.65; by 1973 it had risen by a miniscule amount to 1036.99 and by 1975 it was 1037.42. At the turn of the century the average OG was 1055, which would be considered a very high gravity today. The strongest draught bitter brewed today is Extra Special Bitter from the London independent Fuller, Smith and Turner of Chiswick. It has an OG of 1055.75. Seventy-eight years ago that would have been considered a medium strength beer but today it is popularly known as 'loony juice' or 'kamikaze beer'. Perhaps the most remarkable point about the declining strength of beer is that until the post-second world war period, mild beers outsold bitter. The popularity of bitter is a modern phenomenon. And yet even though bitter has replaced mild, the average OG of beer has fallen dramatically since 1900.

These figures are not an argument in favour of drinking strong beer. There is a lot to be said for drinking low gravity beers, particularly if you intend to drive a car. Low gravity beers tend to be cleaner in taste while high gravity beers can be heavy and rather sweet. A lot depends on your taste and your capacity. I know a man who regularly drinks six pints of Marston's Pedigree (OG 1043) every lunchtime and tops them off with two of Marston's Owd Roger, a ferociously strong old ale with an OG of 1080. He then drives back to his office. The fact that he drives a Rolls-Royce could explain why he has not lost his licence.

The original gravity figures are given to show how beer has got consistently weaker but not cheaper and how this has further enriched the brewers.* The song was right: the brewers *do* water the beer. Adverse publicity has stopped them doing it to their bitters but they have more than got their own back with lager. When the beer giants transformed the industry with national keg brands they started to mine gold. With lager they found Eldorado.

---

*A cool comment on the quality of the Big Six's beer came in April 1976 at the 'Beer Olympics' - the international Brewing Exhibition held in London. Prize for the best draught beer went to Felinfoel of Llanelli. Its Double Dragon won the International Challenge Cup. The company, which has just 80 tied houses, won two other prizes for its beers. Second in the overall championship was Greene King of Bury St Edmunds, for its Abbot Ale. Timothy Taylor of West Yorkshire won first prize for the best mild. Taylor, with only 27 tied houses, also won the championship for the best keg beer: the Big Six could not win anything even in that section. The only big brewery to win a prize in any section were Courage, who came first in a bottled beer section. And in the international bottled lager class, first prizes went to breweries in Mauritius and Togo.

# 6.

# The chill in your glass, the hole in your pocket

*'Lager is an imitation Continental beer drunk only by refined ladies, people with digestive ailments, tourists and other weaklings' — the Munich paper* Suddeutsche Zeitung *commenting in April 1976 on British lager-style beers*

If Britain ever has the misfortune to get sponsored television, there is a good chance that one of the big brewing combines might back a comedy series called Are You Being Conned? It would be concerned with the misadventures of the staff of a large tied public house, complete with limp-wristed barman. One of the running themes of the series would be the way in which the staff use all their considerable powers of verbal and physical persuasion to convince customers that what they really want is keg lager on the grounds that it is cold, Continental, strong and makes you a wow with the ladies and/or the men.

And when they have bamboozled the customers into buying the stuff, the employees go into the back room for a good laugh, knowing that they have actually talked drinkers into forking out for a brew that might be cold but is British-brewed, probably considerably weaker than the draught bitter in the pub and up to 10p a pint dearer. If you would like to see a preview of this programme, then just step into almost any pub in the country, especially during hot weather, and watch the gallons of keg lager disappearing down hundreds of throats. It is a sight that brings delight to the brewing moguls, who have boosted sales of lager from 7 per cent of the market in 1971 to more than 25 per cent in 1977. They confidently expect lager to control 30 per cent of the market by 1980 and 35 per cent by 1985. Even these figures could be drastic underestimates. In the blistering hot weather of 1976 it was thought that lager was controlling up to 40 per cent of the market as the brewers switched ale production around the country to release more capacity for lager brewing. The Whitbread plant at Samlesbury in Lancashire now produces virtually nothing but lager and its new plant in South Wales is planned to produce lager only. Whitbread predict that lager will account for more than half of all beer production by the early 1980s.

One obvious reason for the growth in British lager sales is that many more people now take their holidays abroad and get the taste for the light-coloured chilled beers served there. Many of them are fine beers, pale but pleasant tasting, almost never called lager but bier (lager is the German word for store) and brewed in a quite different manner to traditional British beer. Continental brewers use different malts, different hops and a different yeast which sinks to the bottom of the beer. British beers use yeast that rises to the top during fermentation. As a result of this different brewing process, Continental beers have to be stored for much longer than British beer to allow them to mature and the flavour to develop. The beers are stored or lagered at low temperatures and served chilled.

Many European brewers are skilled craftsmen who, like their British counterparts in the independent companies, struggle to perfect their products. If they ever sampled some of the rubbish served up in Britain as 'lager' they would probably run shrieking to Alcoholics Anonymous. Although some of the European and Scandinavian companies whose beers are brewed under licence in Britain send representatives to keep an eye on quality, a lot of the lager is ersatz stuff, bearing little resemblance to the European model. There is a story, possibly apocryphal, told of a top manager at one of the big lager plants who, when asked if they stored their product in the Continental fashion, replied: 'Store? Why of course we store it - for up to three days.' Three weeks would be a more likely period in Europe or Scandinavia. The story may be an exaggeration but there is little doubt that during the heatwave of 1976 the brewers were churning out lager so fast, often from ill-equipped breweries, that it was just not possible to brew it correctly. There is even some doubt about whether all the brewers bottom-ferment their lager or merely use lighter malts and top ferment the beer to produce something that looks just about right in the glass, even if it tastes wrong in the mouth. And it is hard to tell whether the end product tastes good when its palate is hidden by sub-Arctic temperatures and heavy carbonation. Lager is usually served through a special cooling device called a flash cooler which makes it so cold that it is almost impossible to taste the stuff. British lager is much fizzier than even keg beers because of the high levels of carbonation. On the Continent, even when beer is pressurised, the carbonation levels are usually much lower. Some countries lay down that only a beer's natural carbon dioxide can be used to serve it.

The brewers deny, as always, that they have forced lager on the drinking public. They have merely been following our old friend, demand. Their advertising budgets tell a different story. In 1967 the industry spent just £286,000 promoting lager. By 1974 the budget had increased to £3.2 million. In 1977, out of £20.34 million spent on beer advertising, £9.8 million was devoted to lager. Advertising lager accounted for 48 per cent of promotion budgets, even though lager makes up less than a quarter of total beer sales. Expenditure on lager advertising rose by 49 per cent in 1976 and 1977. The Harp group increased expenditure by 66 per cent. Enormous amounts of money are being thrown around by the combines in a massive propaganda drive to bully more and more drinkers to change to lager. According to the advertisements, it is now difficult or even impossible either to climb a mountain or into bed without the thirst-quenching aid of lager.

Behind the frantic lager drive stands simple, old-fashioned greed. The big brewers exist to make profits and lager, much more than keg beer, is the profit success of the future. The profits are based on the simple ratio of weak beer to high prices. The brewers and their energetic spokesmen at the Brewers' Society counter this by stressing that they have to invest in extra conditioning capacity to store lager while it matures. But that extra cost is offset by the fact that lager usually has a lower original gravity and the companies therefore have to pay less excise duty on it. Stuart Mansell of *The Guardian* took a look at lager in July 1976 and had this to say on the 'extra cost' argument: 'Lager fermentation takes about three weeks compared with one week for most bitters. The valuable fermentation tanks and other capital equipment therefore turn out far less lager, and depreciation per pint must represent a significantly larger sum - but however one does the figure work it's hardly going to be more than 1p a pint more.

'Roughly 1p a pint is also the sum that many brewers save on excise duty because of the lower alcoholic strength of lager. The basic cost of excise duty is £15.84 on a barrel totalling 288 pints of beer with a 1030 original gravity, which is the measure of the beer's strength. For every degree extra the brewer has to pay an extra 58.2p in excise duty. The strength of most ordinary bitters is around 1037, some five points greater than for most standard lagers. So the duty saving on a barrel of lager would be £2.64 or very nearly 1p a pint.' So for the brewer the outlay on producing lager and bitter is the same. It is obvious what happens if they then charge more for lager than bitter.

Mansell found that, apart from Scotland, lager prices were almost always 5p a pint higher than bitter and the differential was as high as 10p in London. His findings were underscored a year later when, after months of painstaking and even painful research, *What's Brewing* compared the gravities and prices of lagers produced by the big companies with bitters of comparable strength. In some cases the paper was unable to compare a company's lager with its bitter. Some lagers had such low gravities that it was forced to compare them with mild ale, often laughingly dismissed as 'an old man's drink'. For example, Bass Charrington's Tuborg has an OG of 1030 (one degree less and it would not even classify as beer) and sold for an average 36p a pint at mid-1977 prices. The Bass subsidiary, Mitchells and Butlers mild, has an OG of 1034 and sold for 25p - 11p a pint cheaper.

A similar pattern is shown if you compare the strengths and prices of the lagers and bitters produced by the independent firms, but the really massive profits are being made by the Big Six, whose lagers control 96 per cent of the market. 29 of the top 65 brewers don't produce their own lager, preferring to take

|  | Original gravity (OG) | Price per pint (pence) |
| --- | --- | --- |
| **Allied Breweries:** | | |
| Skol | 1037 | 36½ |
| Ind Coope bitter | 1037 | 30 |
| Skol Special | 1045 | 41 |
| Burton Ale | 1047 | 37 |
| **Bass Charrington:** | | |
| Tuborg | 1030 | 39 |
| M & B Mild | 1034 | 28 |
| Carling | 1038 | 37 |
| Welsh H.B. | 1037 | 31 |
| **Courage:** | | |
| Harp | 1032 | 36 |
| Mild (Reading) | 1032 | 29 |
| Kronenbourg | 1041 | 41 |
| Best (Reading) | 1039 | 32 |
| **Watney/Carlsberg:** | | |
| Carlsberg | 1031 | 39 |
| Ushers P.A. | 1031 | 28 |
| Carlsberg Hof | 1042 | 42 |
| Trumans Tap | 1039.5 | 37 |
| **Whitbread:** | | |
| Heineken | 1036 | 38 |
| Wethered Trophy | 1035.5 | 31 |
| Stella Artois | 1048 | 45 |
| Brickwoods Best | 1046 | 34 |
| **Scottish & Newcastle:** | | |
| McEwans lager | 1038 | 33 |
| Youngers IPA | 1043 | 31 |

All original gravities and prices are correct at 1 May 1978 and represent countrywide averages in managed and tenanted public bars.

the products of the combines - though it is not always a question of preference. Of the nine companies in which Whitbread hold more than 10 per cent of the shares, six sell Whitbread's Heineken. Three of the four companies in which Bass have a major stake serve mainly Bass lagers.

A firm of City of London stockbrokers estimated in 1977 that profit margins on lager were double those on other beers. When the marketing director of the Northern Federation Clubs co-operative brewery was asked what he thought of the prices charged by the Big Six for lager, he exploded with rage and said: 'They're the biggest con ever in the brewing industry.' Northern Clubs brews its own lager and charged 25p a pint in 1977.

British lager is a double con. The consumers are not only helping the brewers to make fat profits from lager now but are also being forced to pay for investment in lager so that even bigger profits can be made in the future. As the Price Commission found, rather than borrow on a long term basis, the brewers are funding their investment by charging 'what the market will stand' for lager. £1 billion was due to be spent between 1977 and 1980 on major capital investment, much of it on building new lager or mainly lager fizz factories such as Whitbread's at Magor and Courage's in Berkshire. As the Brewers' Society put it, more than 70 per cent of the money for this investment programme will be 'generated from within the industry' - in other words, from profits.

The drinkers are being conned in a third way: the style of advertising and the brand names used both suggest that the lagers on sale in Britain are genuine Continental or Scandinavian brews. In fact all the 'draught' lagers sold in Britain are brewed in this country. The ones that carry the same names as famous foreign beers are brewed here under licence. They are not the same beers, though. When *What's Brewing* tested the original gravities of Dutch Heineken and Whitbread Heineken, it found that the Dutch version had an OG of 1048.6 and the British rated 1033. There is also considerable difference in taste. Although it is a pressurised beer, Dutch Heineken has a light, clean taste while to my tastebuds British Heineken, like most British ersatz lager, tastes like cold metal polish.

The consumers may be kidded by advertising and expensive bar mountings into thinking they are drinking something excitingly Scandinavian or German but, in spite of such names as Carlsberg, Norseman, Viking, Tuborg, Grunhalle (a Gothicised version of Greenall), Brock, which supplements Hall and Woodhouse's Badger beer and, most ludicrous of all, Hibrau from Guernsey, most British-brewed lagers are as European or Scandinavian as Chipping Sodbury on a wet Thursday.

The tragedy and the scandal of British lagers is that nothing is done about them. There is now sufficient evidence to show that lager is wickedly over-priced but no action is taken at government level, apart from knuckle-rapping from the Price Commission. The battle against keg beer has to a large extent been won. Sales of the major brands are on the slide. But the great lager circus rolls on, carrying us to the brave new world where everyone will drink Euro-fizz. It is a chilling prospect.

# 7.
# Nasty bits

*'The American brewing industry, the world's greatest beer polluter, seems determined to maintain that role with the announcement of an innovation by the giant Jos. Schlitz company. The system, known as Active Balanced Fermentation, uses paddles and stirrers to agitate fermenting beer violently. The normal mechanism of fermentation is broken. All the yeast is kept in suspension and the liquid ferments more rapidly. 'We've given the traditional art of brewing a helping hand,' claimed Wilhelm C. Janssen, vice-president of seven Schlitz plants, 'and in return we're getting the assurance of greater uniformity and quality. Nature is not the best brewmaster — there are inconsistencies in her way. The Active Balanced Fermentation is a distinct improvement on nature'.'* — What's Brewing, *March 1976*

In June 1976 I asked Peter Scully, head brewer at Tolly Cobbold in Ipswich, whether he used potatoes, onions, and pasta flour to help brew his beers. 'A certain amount of refined starch can be used - and potato produces refined starch,' he replied. But did he actually use potatoes? 'We are perfectly capable of using potatoes,' he said. I told Mr Scully that with such an ability to deflect awkward questions he should have been a politician, not a brewer.

Members of the Campaign for Real Ale had earlier returned from visits to Tolly with alarming rumours that potato starch, pasta flour and even onions were being used in the brew.

Though Mr Scully neither admitted nor denied this, he did tell me that he used 15 per cent wheat as an adjunct to the malted barley. The sacks of pasta flour have now disappeared from the Tolly brewery and they assure me that they 'no longer' use potato starch, but Mr Scully no doubt continues to use wheat adjunct. He is not alone in this practice. The use of adjuncts and malt substitutes have become a major problem in recent years and some of the beer brewed in Britain would not be classified as such in countries that have strict laws governing its production. In Germany, a medieval law called the Reinheitsgebot, which stipulates that beer for home consumption may be brewed only from malted barley, hops, water and yeast, is still in force. The Isle of Man has a similar Pure Beer Law. In Britain there is no such legislation and brewers can use what they like to replace malted barley. Sometimes the nitrogen content of barley can be affected by the weather before harvesting and this needs to be adjusted if the flavour of the beer is to remain constant. But the overriding reason why the chemists who have replaced traditional brewers in the big combines now use such adjuncts as malt extract, hop extract, flaked maize and rice grits is that they are cheaper than natural barley and hops. They also have a distinct and detrimental effect on the final palate of the beer.

In 1977 the European Economic Community's Beer Commission was forced to drop a draft beer directive that sought to harmonise the production of beer brewed for export between one Common Market country and another. It would not have affected the brewing of beer for consumption within member countries, but the directive produced such a howl of rage from the German brewing industry that the Brussels bureaucrats were forced to spike their plans. The Germans objected because the directive would have allowed up to 40 per cent of non-malted material to have been used in the brewing process, including other cereals and rice. The directive would also have allowed hop extract to be used instead of natural hops. The Germans were outraged because they could see only too clearly that cheap beers using inferior ingredients could flood their market and undermine the strict Reinheitsgebot. The result would have been that less scrupulous German brewers would have followed suit and the quality of German beer - and much of it is unprocessed and of exceptional quality - would begin to slide.

Beer using flaked maize and rice grits may not taste as good as beer brewed from traditional ingredients but they will probably do you no harm. It is the use of chemicals in beer that is more worrying. The same EEC draft directive would have allowed the following 'production aids': industrial enzymes, foam stabilisers, beer stabilisers, anti-oxidants, giberellic acid and taurocholic acid. The fact that such 'aids' were to be allowed by the EEC indicates that they are widely used already in the brewing industry. Many brewers are known to use formaldehyde, a preservative for dead bodies and a fitting substance to help produce the dead, sterile keg beers that pass for beer today.

One chemical not permitted in the now-defunct EEC directive, but widely used in Britain, is silicone anti-foam, which contains an active polymer called polydimethyl siloxane. Brewers were keen to use it to prevent a thick, yeasty head forming during fermentation. If the head could be cut down, they reasoned, then they could get more liquid into the fermenting vessels and improve production and profits. The big brewers rushed to use antifoam and argued that the chemicals would be lost when the beer was filtered and fined. But traces of antifoam were discovered when the beer was ready to leave the breweries. Some of the brewers immediately stopped using it but others did not, as there was no law against it. Which means that the pint in your hand could contain minute traces of polydimethyl siloxane.

It could also contain HHB, short for n-heptyl-p-hydroxy benzoate, used first in America and adopted with some fervour by the big British brewers. The Americans were concerned that the cost of the plant to pasteurise bottled and kegged beer was prohibitive. Pasteurisation also left a tell-tale tang to the beer that many drinkers found disagreeable. The brewers came to the conclusion that it would be easier, cut down on space and would therefore be cost-effective and more profitable to add a chemical preservative to the beer that would effectively kill it and prevent any build up of bacteria. Two preservatives were tried: para-hydroxy-amino-benzoate and octyl-gallate. They were taken up in Britain until it was discovered that the preservatives left a slight haze in the beer, which ruined the marketing people's image of a crystal clear glass of keg. The brewers switched to HHB, which was also being tested in America, and found to be more effective than the other preservatives and left the beer free from haze. In 1972 toxicological investigations on HHB with rats found some evidence of biological build-up and accumulation of the chemical in the tissues. The results were inconclusive and the technical committee of the Brewers' Society decided to give HHB their seal of approval. The soft drinks industry, most of which is owned by the Big Six, is also investigating the use of HHB. In the meantime, the British Industrial Biological Research Association is looking into the toxicological effects that preservatives such as HHB might have. But even if their findings throw serious doubts on their use in food and drink, there is still no legislation to outlaw them.

Chemicals are used in beer not to make them safer or better but simply as a marketing device. If the promotion departments of the brewing monopolies decide that the public, especially young people of both sexes and women of all ages, who are not great beer drinkers, must be brainwashed into accepting their notion of the perfect pint, then chemicals and preservatives are added to make beer and lager fit that notion. I have even heard it said that when one of the big companies was drawing up plans for a new beer, the accountants argued for low gravity and a high price in order to make good profits. The marketing people insisted that the beer should be strong as they were going to promote it with a strong 'he-man' image. The problem was passed to the chemists. The gravity of the beer was kept low but chemicals were added so that after a few pints drinkers would wake up the next morning with a blinding headache and convince themselves - and their friends - that they must have had an exceptionally strong beer the night before.

Chemical additives can give you more than just a sore head. In America, where monopolisation and the processing of beer have gone even further than in Britain, the brewers started to use cobalt sulphate to inject a lively head to the beer. More than 40 people died of heart attacks after drinking cobalt beer and its use was banned. Other ingredients may not be so lethal but until a full investigation has been made there is a powerful life-or-death argument in favour of their withdrawal.

Asbestos is another cause for concern. Beers that are bottled, kegged or turned into 'bright' beer are filtered, often through asbestos sheet. Both the Asbestos Advisory Committee and the Food Additives and Contaminates Committee are studying the effects of asbestos. The government sponsored Asbestos Information Committee has said there is no evidence that swallowing a small amount of asbestos fibre will cause any harm. It rather depends on what is considered to be 'a small amount'. Answering a question on the use of asbestos filters in brewing, in the House of Lords in 1977, a government spokesman said that the average pint of beer contained 5,000 fibres. In the Commons, Junior Agriculture Minister Gavin Strang told a questioner that the incidence of asbestos fibre was no greater in beer filtered through asbestos than in unfiltered beer. The Brewers' Society also feel there is no cause for concern, and a spokesman told me that a glass of water contained as much asbestos fibre from the atmosphere as a glass of beer. But Patrick Kinnersly, author of *The Hazards of Work*, is opposed to such complacency and points out that asbestos fibres migrate through the tissue walls into the bloodstream. Until the current research into asbestos is completed, an adage good enough for journalism should be good enough for brewing: if in doubt, leave it out.

New production methods also threaten the palate of beer. Bass have been experimenting with a process called continuous fermentation - pioneered, of course, in the United States - in which liquid passes endlessly through a high concentration of yeast in closed, conical fermenters, instead of being left to ferment naturally for several days in open fermenting vessels. Other companies are trying a process called high gravity brewing. Beer is brewed to a high gravity and is then watered down with special deaerated and pasteurised water to suit local recipes, after being trunked around the country. As the production development manager of Bass Charrington, Kenneth Skinner, admitted in a lecture in 1977, this process can have a distinct effect on the palate of the beer, rendering it bland and lacking in flavour. But the process has its appeal. Brewers can utilise their plant to great cost effectiveness if one high gravity brew is used to produce several different beers when it is watered down.

Beer drinkers have been kept in the dark by the brewers about the ingredients and the methods they use, but a major stride towards greater consumer knowledge came in March 1977 with the report of the Ministry of Agriculture's Food Standards Committee, which had beavered away for three years on the composition and labelling of beer. It is a remarkable fact that the law now requires manufacturers to list the ingredients in a can of soup or a tin of baked beans but no such requirements are demanded of the brewers. The FSC report was anxious to change this situation. It said that 'the composition, labelling and advertising of beer should be subject to the same kind of legislation control as many other foods.' Sadly, the committee dodged the issue of beer additives. It said the prohibition of additives, urged on it by CAMRA, was not realistic and shuffled the problem sideways to the Food Additives and Contaminants Committee.

While CAMRA were also critical of the FSC for not recommending a minimum malt content for beer and for failing to distinguish sufficiently between pressurised and unpressurised beer, there was general pleasure at the fact that, if the report's recommendations were eventually accepted by the government, beer drinkers would know a lot more about their beer than at present. Bulk beer would be labelled 'cask conditioned' or 'bulk conditioned' and the dispensers for heavily carbonated beers would be marked 'carbon dioxide exceeds 1.5 volumes'. Some indication of the strength of beer would be given by the X-rating system, and the percentages of barley malt and other cereals would be declared.

The Ministry of Agriculture has asked for comments on the report from all interested parties and there is no timetable for the possible enactment of the final recommendations. It is to be hoped that this report will not end up on another shelf through lack of parliamentary time or government unwillingness to displease the big brewers. And the brewers are displeased. They were lukewarm to the FSC all along and have said that beer drinkers do not want to be bothered by too much information about their beer. At least they are consistent: the big brewers have always claimed that they know what the drinkers' want. Now they claim to know what the drinkers do not want to know.

Just in case the FSC report should some day pass into law, the brewers have an old method of getting their own back on the consumers. If they have to print all this information, they declared in 1977, then inevitably the price of beer would rise as a result.

# 8.

# Blowing off the froth

*'Size has not been the main reason for our success. Ind Coope have put Burton Ale into 600 pubs. They didn't come and inspect our membership files. We convinced them that tens of thousands of people would drink it.' — Michael Hardman, founder member of CAMRA*

The Campaign for Real Ale started in an inconsequential way. Four men, Mellor, Makin, Hardman and Lees, were on holiday in Ireland, enjoying the Irish Guinness and, as people do in pubs, bemoaning the quality and price of British beer. From that impromptu discussion there developed a powerful consumer movement that now has 22,000 members, has restored traditional draught beer to many thousands of pubs, and has literally shaken one big brewing combine, Watney Mann & Truman, from top to bottom. The movement was described in 1976 by Michael Young, then chairman of the National Consumer Council, as 'the most successful consumer movement in Europe'.

When they started in 1971, Mellor, Makin, Hardman and Lees didn't even know the difference between keg beer and real draught beer. They just knew that they didn't like the taste of the new, heavily-promoted gassy stuff or the price they were forced to pay for it. They decided to form an organisation called the Campaign for the Revitalisation of Ale. Michael Hardman became chairman, Graham Lees secretary, Jim Makin treasurer and Bill Mellor organiser. Then they went on with their holiday, returned home and did no more about the campaign. 'It was more a gesture of hope than a planned assault on the brewing

75

citadels,' Hardman said.

Lees, Hardman and Mellor were journalists. They got around a lot, drank a lot, talked to people in pubs and at work, and found they were not alone. There were thousands of people who thought like them and wanted to do something about beer. Gradually an organisation started to take shape, with its head-quarters first at Graham Lees' mother's flat in Salford, later in Lees' own flat in St Albans where he was working on the local evening paper and kept membership records in an old shoe box. A small monthly paper called *What's Brewing* was typed and Letrasetted by the founders in their spare time and a conference was called in 1972. About 100 people attended, took away membership cards and began to spread the word.

Hardman and Lees were busy learning about beer. They talked their way into breweries big and small, and rapidly acquired a knowledge of the brewing process that was invaluable if they were to be taken seriously by the big breweries. *What's Brewing* published articles that told consumers for the first time how their beer was brewed, the additives that were often used and how processed and pressurised keg beers were produced. Technical matters such as original gravity and excise duty were explained so that readers could see how to get value for their money, and how the brewing conglomerates saved theirs by watering down their beer. Drinkers were being informed for the first time in brewing history, and the brewers didn't like it. They dismissed CAMRA as irrelevant but the irrelevance wouldn't go away. It was now the Campaign for Real Ale (some members had complained that it was hard to get the tongue round 'revitalisation', especially after a few pints) and volunteer members were badgering brewers and talking to drinkers and landlords about the need to restore choice to pubs by having traditional beer alongside the kegs. In some pubs, landlords found long forgotten beer engines in their cellars, wiped away the cobwebs, put them back in the bar and asked their breweries to start supplying cask-conditioned beer again. The revolution was under way.

The Campaign was becoming more professional. Michael Hardman recalls: 'We were lucky to pick up some notables who had waged their own small campaign to find real ale pubs or to save small breweries. There was John Hanscomb, with a great knowledge of brewing and beer, who edited the first *Good Beer Guide*, Andrew Cunningham, a mine of information on pubs, who had drunk every brew in Britain save one, Frank Baillie (author of the *Beer Drinker's Companion*), who had drunk in almost every pub in the country, and Chris Hutt, who was writing *Death of the English Pub* and who became the second chairman of CAMRA.'

The brewers had claimed that they knew what drinkers wanted and were merely following public demand by phasing out real ale and replacing it with keg beer. The growth of CAMRA proved their stance to be false. Between 1973 and 1974, the Campaign's membership grew from 1,000 to close on 10,000. When Richard Boston mentioned CAMRA and its address in his *Guardian* column, letters poured in to the Campaign's part-time office from all parts of the country. A full time secretary was appointed and offices were rented above a cycle shop in St Albans. Beer drinkers were starting to find their voices and were telling the brewers that they didn't like their processed beers, and wanted the real thing back.

Hardman came to work full time for the Campaign and used his considerable professional flair to run CAMRA's publications. *What's Brewing* became a monthly tabloid newspaper, the *Good Beer Guide* was established as a successful annual selection of some of the best real ale pubs (it sold 70,000 copies in 1977) and the press were bombarded with press releases sounding off against the big brewers and their fizzy beers.

The journalistic experience of leading members like Hardman and Lees was vital to the early success of CAMRA. They had the journalist's gift for catching the media's attention. When a London beer exhibition said it would sell only keg beers and refused to allow another and much smaller real ale group, the Society for the Preservation of Beer from the Wood, to have a stand at the exhibition, CAMRA members paraded outside with banners, placards and a coffin representing the death of traditional beer. When Courage and John Smith announced the closure of Barnsley Brewery, CAMRA marched through the town with a band, and local MP Roy Mason at their head. When Bass closed Joules brewery, CAMRA members organised a funeral and, dressed as undertakers, delivered wreaths to the brewery.

The press loved it and soon the name CAMRA became a talking point in pubs and breweries. When Bill Tidy started to draw a regular cartoon for *What's Brewing* called Keg Buster, a chronicle of the adventures of a flat-capped, whippet-fancying northerner who detested fizzy ale, he coined the name 'Grotny' for a certain national brewery combine. The name stuck and appeared on thousands of T-shirts. There was never a specific anti-Watney initiative by CAMRA but the derision for that company's keg products implicit in Tidy's play on words was to dent Watney's image badly, as it was later to admit, and force it to change its brewing policies. Keg Buster was later to immortalise another combine as 'Twitbreads'. The signs are that even that most hostile of companies is beginning to rethink its attitude to beer.

CAMRA spread its wings. A separate company called CAMRA (Real Ale) Investments was set up, with Christopher Hutt as company secretary, to buy a small number of real ale pubs and act as a model for the industry. When the first 250,000 shares were offered for sale, the money to buy the first two pubs was raised within weeks and the share issue was heavily oversubscribed. The venture has not been entirely successful. The company bought five pubs in quick succession and spent a lot of money in renovating them, with the result that heavy losses were made in its first two years of trading though it recorded a small profit for 1977. It has found, as have many other free houses, that the overheads of running only a few pubs are high and consequently their prices are not as sharply competitive as many CAMRA members would like. The siting of some of the pubs, particularly one in Hampstead, has not been popular with CAMRA members who feel the company should be selling real ale in the Norfolk and Northampton beer deserts and not to middle-class trendies who have plenty of other pubs to choose from. When Michael Hardman left CAMRA's full time staff in 1977 he told *What's Brewing* that, with the benefit of hindsight, he thought CAMRA Investments had been a mistake. 'We'd always thought of running model pubs and I was 100 per cent in favour of CAMRA Investments at the time. But a consumer organisation shouldn't run pubs. It ought to stand apart from the business it is criticising and analysing. We can't be critical of other pubs if we are running our own.'

By 1975-76, membership of the Campaign had swollen to 30,000 and the demands on the tiny full time staff were becoming impossible. Bigger premises were found in St Albans, a full time campaign administrator was hired to sort out the confusion created by the influx of hundreds of new members every week and extra journalistic and secretarial staff were taken on.

The Campaign has been a victim of its own success. Membership slipped back to 25,000 in 1977 and a major financial crisis was averted by doubling the subscription to £4 a year, but with a further loss of members. It seems likely that membership will settle down to around 20,000 with a high turnover. Many people join for a year, think they know all there is to know about beer and drop out. Others are swayed by the proliferation of new cask-conditioned beers into thinking that the battle has been won, and they become inactive. But the more far-sighted members know that while membership is important it is not size alone that has helped to keep back the tide of fizzy beer: CAMRA convinced the brewers there was a substantial market for traditional beer. CAMRA's unusual form of organisation, making it more like a political party or a trade union than a typical consumer group, added to its effectiveness.

Britain's consumer movement was attacked by Nicholas Faith in the *Sunday Times* in 1977. He described it as providing jobs for otherwise unemployable members of the middle class. More brutal criticism came from Polly Toynbee in *The Guardian* in December 1977 when she compared the lavish budgets and swank offices of the official consumer watchdog groups with their general lack of impact. Most consumer groups are purely passive. If your gas cooker is badly installed, you can get in touch with the Gas Users' Council who will look into the problem for you. But it will not go out and campaign to make sure that all gas cookers are correctly installed. The Consumers Association, publishers of *Which?*, are enthusiastically concerned with the quality of freezers, hi-fis, dish washers and washing machines, which makes them somewhat remote from the sizeable section of the community which cannot afford these things.

CAMRA is different because it is an organisation which responds quickly, with definite action. If it had merely recorded the disparate grumbles of the nation's beer drinkers, Britain would still be awash in Double Diamond and Carlsberg lager, with scarcely a drop of the real stuff to be found. The Campaign was set up as a radical organisation that would take the fight to the brewers. Its members are organised into 150 branches and, as well as a full time staff of eight, it has voluntary branch secretaries, and area and regional organisers. Its image is rather different from that drawn by its critics, who portray CAMRA as made up either of drunken, beer-bellied oafs or beer bores muttering about the nitrogen content and hop rate of their ale. The Campaign has a fair number of both, but in the main it is sustained by dedicated members working hard to keep the central organisation functioning. They organise local meetings with breweries, beer festivals with a wide range of brews, and socials in pubs that stock real ale - or would like to if the brewery would supply it. CAMRA has regional conferences and an annual meeting, which discuss a wide range of motions on such matters as how to tackle the more intransigent of the brewing combines, liberalising the licensing laws, fighting price rises in general and the more outrageous prices charged for both trendy real ales and weak lager. They also campaign for maintaining public bars in pubs so that those on lower incomes can still get a comparatively cheap pint.

The Campaign has its problems. Although it has strong branches in Greater Manchester and Merseyside and growing ones in the north-east and Scotland, it remains predominantly southern-based and middle class in composition. It has yet to make big gains among the working-class section of the drinking population, who could add much-needed muscle to the fight against the brewers. CAMRA is also male-dominated and has just one woman on its national executive. This is less a criticism of the Campaign and more a reflection of the fact that pubs have for long been bastions of male supremacy, although this situation is now breaking down, particularly in the south.

Funds are still the major problem. The Campaign has

always been under-financed. The original subscription was five shillings a year and it crept up to 50p, £1 and £2. The decision in 1976 to peg the membership fee at £2 for two years was a disaster. It was a time of roaring inflation. As the cost of postage and telephones soared, CAMRA rapidly ran up a £15,000 bank overdraft and one of its most accomplished chairmen, Chris Bruton, spent most of his time in office warding off the bank and the creditors while the staff hoped their pay cheques would not bounce. A £1 associate membership scheme has been launched to complement the full £4 subscription in an attempt to win more members, but financial worries are far from over.

The Campaign can be over serious. In 1977 there was a real possibility that CAMRA might split and disintegrate as a row simmered for months over an obscure doctrinal issue concerning beer served by air pressure. Air pressure dispense is rarely used in England and Wales but it is the traditional method for serving draught beer in Scotland where either water engines or electric compressors are used. CAMRA turned a blind eye to this different method and allowed Scottish pubs using air pressure to be included in the *Good Beer Guide*. Then Truman put the casks among the kegs in 1977 by introducing a real beer, Tap bitter, in the south-east, dispensed by a new air pressure system invented by the Distillers Company, best known to beer drinkers for supplying gas cylinders for keg pubs. CAMRA's National Executive decided, rather pompously, that air pressure could not be allowed in England because the air trapped inside the cask would act in the same way as a blanket covering of carbon dioxide gas. The beer could not breathe and would become fizzy, they said. To be consistent, they also decided that Scottish pubs using air pressure would also be outlawed from the *Good Beer Guide*.

The Scottish branches were deeply affronted and threatened to split from the national body. The row went on for month after month in the pages of *What's Brewing* and the more technically-minded of its members produced carbonation tables and other scientific evidence to prove or disprove their point. In the end, an emergency conference decided to permit air pressure dispense, but to give discretion to branches as to whether to allow air pressure pubs from their localities to appear in the

*Good Beer Guide.* Scotland was happy and the split was healed. But CAMRA had lost face during the row. The brewers could sit back and laugh as their major critic threatened to tear itself in two, and the scientific mumbo-jumbo of much of the debate showed how remote the Campaign could be from its erstwhile supporters in thousands of public bars and saloons throughout the country.

That is the debit side. The credit side is stronger. But for CAMRA's existence, traditional beer would not exist in large areas of the country. London is a good example. In the early 1970s it was called a beer desert. It was true that many Charrington pubs sold the firm's IPA in real form, but apart from those and a handful of pubs owned by the independents, Youngs and Fullers, every Watney and Truman house and most of Courage and Whitbread offered only pressurised beer. Now real ale is widely available in 1,500 pubs. The free trade is buoyant with beer from regional companies such as Ruddles, Samuel Smiths, Adnams, Brakspears, Shepherd Neame, Eldridge Pope, Marstons and Arkell. Courage were on the verge of phasing out their famous Directors Bitter a few years ago but its sales are booming and it is being brewed in Bristol now as well as London. (An interesting taste comparison between real beer and keg can be made by drinking Directors Bitter and John Courage 'draught': they are the same brew except that some is put into casks and allowed to mature properly while the rest is chilled, filtered and pasteurised for the keg form.)

Whitbread have introduced the fine-tasting Marlow bitter from the old Thomas Wethered brewery into a number of London outlets, and Watney and Truman, which had ceased to brew cask beer at all, are now producing Fined Bitter and Tap bitter. When Scottish and Newcastle brought Younger's Scotch bitter back to the capital in December 1977, the Big Six were once again all serving cask beer in London.

St Albans, where CAMRA has its headquarters, had just one pub serving real ale when Graham Lees came to work in the town in 1972. The pub, the Farriers Arms, sold McMullen's mild. Lees convinced the licensee, George Vardy, an expatriate Cockney with a ribald sense of humour, to also serve McMullen's excellent Country Bitter. Vardy was sceptical but he put the beer on and found he could hardly shut the pub doors because of the rush of business. Nevertheless, the message was slow to spread. When I came to work for CAMRA in February 1976 there were still only three pubs in the town serving draught beer. Today there are 30. As a result of Ind Coope's near monopoly of pubs in the town it is nearly all Burton Ale and Ind Coope bitter, but they have been joined by Bass, Greene King, Whitbread, Sam Smith, Courage and Charles Wells.

Other areas have prospered in a similar way but there is still a lot to be done. Vast tracts of Scotland have nothing but pressurised beer from S & N and Tennents. The north-east, Northamptonshire and Norfolk are still desperately short of choice. It is absurd that S & N can bring Younger's real beer down to London to jostle with a wide range of other cask beer but the company cannot supply it to drinkers on their own doorstep in Scotland and Tyneside.

There have been dramatic changes inside the industry. Watney - which once emulated Henry Ford by telling their publicans that they could have their houses painted any colour they liked, as long as it was red - have decentralised with a rapid, embarrassed shuffle. The company has been split into nine mainly autonomous regional companies, and famous names such as Wilsons, Ushers and Websters have re-emerged from under the layers of red paint and ugly white lettering. Truman has been disentangled from Watney and has been given a degree of independence. Watney pubs are now being repainted any colour but red to avoid the infamous image.

A report by Watney's own stockbrokers and City advisers, Panmure Gordon, admitted in 1976 that Watney had misread consumer resistance to keg beer and the combine had suffered as a result: 'There can be little doubt that trade in Watney public houses was adversely affected by CAMRA and various beer and pub guides. Watney was the easiest target in the industry ... Some commentators have also pointed out that the public houses, particularly in the London area, were perhaps more easily recognisable than those belonging to other brews. The exterior decor, featuring white lettering on a cherry-coloured background, stands out prominently, though older, less garish styles are still to be seen in some areas. A Watney pub, it is suggested, has been easy to identify and consequently easy to avoid, if the customer is determined to do so.' It speaks volumes about the state of the brewing industry when Watney's financial advisers can suggest that the firm's prominence and easy recognition were a bar to commercial success. As Watney now paint their pubs green, blue and grey, they also tacitly admit that the great 'red revolution' beer has not been an overwhelming success. Watney's Red is being replaced by Ben Truman Export and more than 300 London and south-east pubs now stock Watney's new cask beer, Fined Bitter. The name Mann's has re-emerged and Mann's cask-conditioned bitter is available in the West Midlands. Three more cask beers from Watney were due to appear in 1978. Strangely, though, Fined Bitter is brewed in Norwich and trunked to London. Not a drop of it is allowed to reach the ale lovers in Norfolk.

Allied Breweries have also genuflected to CAMRA. In July 1976, Ind Coope introduced a new cask beer called Burton Ale and even promoted it with a certain amount of razzmatazz. Nearly a thousand pubs south of Burton-upon-Trent now stock Burton Ale and 'supersite' billboards advertise the beer in London. The beer has met with considerable success and sales of Ind Coope's ordinary bitter and mild also seem to be improving. In 1977 Allied followed Watney and announced a major reorganisation that would give greater freedom to the individual companies and would allow the almost forgotten Walker beers in Warrington to reappear, while several new cask beers were promised for 1978. Allied have not denied that sales of Double Diamond are falling fast. A popular drinkers' badge mocked that brand's advertising style with the slogan 'DD is K9P'; perhaps it will soon be replaced by one saying 'DD RIP'.

The future is not so rosy where Courage and Whitbread are concerned. The rescue of Courage's Directors Bitter from oblivion has been offset by the closure of Barnsley and the threat that the new Berkshire Brewery will produce only pressurised beer. And while Whitbread have allowed the Marlow brewery to expand sales of its cask beer, the closure of the Rhymney and Blackburn breweries in 1978 placed a question mark over several older breweries under the Whitbread umbrella.

Bass Charrington, king of the kegs, claim that they brew

more cask beer than all the other brewers in Britain, and possibly Europe, put together. It is probably true and points to the frightening dominance of the conglomerate. Some of their beers are magnificent - there are few better ales around than draught Bass - but others like Brew Ten and Extra Light are mediocre products. Overall, less than a quarter of Bass's production is real draught beer and fizz farms like the multi-million Runcorn plant are frightening previews of what the future might be if the big brewers have their way.

At the other end of the scale, the independent companies are booming. While some keep their distance from CAMRA, others, like Ruddles, cheerfully admit that without the presence of the Campaign they would have been struggling to survive in recent years. CAMRA has not only opened up the market for real beer, it has also created a climate in which it would be more difficult for the giants to go on the takeover trail again, though the financial stake that Whitbread have in firms such as Ruddles, Marstons and Boddingtons is a cause for concern.

A number of smaller companies were about to jump on the keg bandwagon in the early 1960s until the real ale revival warned them off. Fullers in West London had worked out elaborate plans to convert their old Griffin brewery to pressurised production when they sniffed the wind, changed tack and reaped a rich reward. In south London, Youngs of Wandsworth turned their backs on processed beer and went on brewing as they had been taught to do. John Young, their ebullient chairman, loves to tell the story of a meeting of the Brewers' Society in the 1960s when, during a break in proceedings, the members noticed a hearse passing the building. 'There goes another of your customers, John,' one of the big brewers' representatives said to Young, and the other keg men fell about laughing. They would not dare to laugh in his presence now. The demand for Young's beer is so great that the brewery cannot keep up, and the free trade and beer festivals have to go without Young's ales while the company struggles to supply its own tied houses.

While the future of traditional beer seems assured, there is no room for complacency. A report by stockbrokers Rowe and Pitman in October 1977 suggested that sales of real ale were falling and would be cut by half in the next five years. Some CAMRA members dismissed the claims as propaganda from the big brewers' 'dirty tricks' departments and the proposition does seem absurd. Rowe and Pitman were dealing only with the production of the Big Six and they did not distinguish between genuine cask-conditioned beer and that served by gas pressure. In 1977, 18 new real ales came on to the market, five new small breweries started up and there seems to be no slackening in demand for traditional beer. But, as we have seen, even when a firm such as Ruddles doubles its production in successive years, those figures scarcely show on the overall production graph. The forecast of Rowe and Pitman could be right if the accountants in the Big Six were to decide that the proportion of the market that goes to cask beer - currently 14 per cent -was too small to warrant its continued production.

Action is more important than speculation, however. But for the activities of a militant consumer movement, traditional beer would certainly have disappeared from most parts of the country. Its future survival depends on a continuing high level of activity. It is true that CAMRA have won the keg beer battle but sales of lager are still growing at an alarming pace. Unless that is countered and steps are taken to break the grip of the combines, real ale enthusiasts could find their supplies cut off by the ice-floes.

# 9.

# An all-bright tomorrow?

*'It has been clear ever since its introduction that "New Smoking Material" (sawdust to its friends) is a commercial flop ... Imperial Group, owners of NSM, are not deterred by the failure of their attempts to synthesise fags and are now extending the notion to other areas of their business. Their brewing subsidiary Courage is going ahead with plans to introduce "New Drinking Material" at a multi-million-pound plant at Worton Grange near Reading.' — Newsletter of the mid-Chilterns branch of CAMRA*

The brewing industry is in crisis. Consumers are unhappy with the choice of beer. Official bodies are concerned by the near total monopoly exercised by the Big Six. Some experts believe that the combines have over-reacted to the demand for lager and think that its sales may soon level off, leaving many breweries with extra capacity in a few years. Others take the opposite view and feel that lager will come to dominate the market in a few years time and that all other beers will disappear; Britain, despite its temperate climate, will have to follow the rest of the world in drinking light, chilled beer.

The vandalism of the early 1970s, recorded graphically by Christopher Hutt, has receded to some extent. While many pubs are still tarted up in the most revolting manner, public bars ripped out and traditional games replaced by pool tables and television ping-pong, the brewers have calmed down some of their more enthusiastic architectural desperadoes and have left some of their pubs in traditional form.

87

But the number of pubs is declining by more than 300 a year and close on 10,000 pubs have closed since the end of the last world war. Some rationalisation was necessary. The time when every street had one or two pubs could not survive television and the supermarket. But now there are worrying signs that the rationalisation has gone too far. Many rural areas have no pubs at all and, as we have seen in Norfolk, community life has been badly hurt.

The problem stems from the domination of the giant brewers. At the end of the takeover scramble, the combines found themselves with thousands of pubs, many of them in outlying areas at the end of long delivery runs. Many required substantial amounts of money to bring them up to standard. Whitbread and Courage have led the field in disposing of pubs. In 1976 Whitbread got rid of 250, 3 per cent of their tied pubs, and more go on the market every year. Between 1976 and 1977, Courage disposed of 150 pubs and a spokesman said: 'Smaller pubs are not giving a return on investment. They need modernisation but we can't justify spending £5,000-£10,000 on them.' No sign there of social responsibility, of providing a service to many hard-pressed areas and to consumers who pay inflated prices for their beer. Although they are the hubs of many communities, pubs are dismissed as 'not giving a return on investment'.

When a rural pub is closed it usually stays so. In towns, some are snapped up by the free trade and pubs offering a wide variety of beers start to offer some competition to the Big Six houses. But still the big brewers chuckle all the way to the bank. In Bristol, for example, where Courage have sold pubs and lost trade to free houses, they are still making big profits from their remaining estates. Alan Robinson-Wildman is the chairman of the Bristol Licensed Victuallers Association and he has seen at close hand the way in which Courage operate. They have been savagely increasing the rents they charge their tenants. In one case, at the end of a normal three-year contract, Courage put up the rent of a pub from £600 a year to £2,200, leaving the landlord and his wife with an annual income of £1,400. Rent increases of as much as £3,280 a year have been recorded by the Bristol LVA. In November 1977 Mr Robinson-Wildman lobbied Prices Secretary Roy Hattersley on behalf of Avon tenants, telling the government minister that Courage were 'squeezing the life out of small pubs'. He said that Courage charged high rents while subsidising their own managed houses and giving interest-free loans to clubs and the free trade. He claimed that managed pubs in Bristol, often with better facilities, undercut tenanted houses by 2p a pint. He demanded government action to keep the smaller tenanted pubs in operation.

Justice can be equally rough when a brewery decides to close a pub. One of the major jobs of the National Union of Licensed Victuallers, to which LVAs are affiliated, is to get adequate compensation for its members when they face eviction. In 1976 the NULV reported the case of a Courage tenant in Kent who was offered £860 compensation plus £700 for furniture and fittings after 18 years in the pub. The tenant offered to buy the pub from Courage for £38,000 but the offer was rejected and the pub was sold over his head for £45,000. The NULV's files bulge with similar distressing stories.

Evictions were at their height in the late 1960s during the period of rent freeze. Thousands of tenants were thrown out of their jobs and homes and replaced by managers, employed directly by the brewing companies. The reasoning was that with rents frozen, profits from the tied estate would have to be raised by paying low wages to pub managers. The plan backfired. The managers organised themselves into a small but tough union, the National Association of Licensed House Managers, who set out to boost their wages from a derisory £650 in 1968 to more than £3,000 a year by 1978. The brewers retreated and rethought their tactics. The swing to managed houses stopped in the mid-1970s and profits from the tied estate are now being made by a combination of property disposal and heavily increased rents for tenants.

The Big Six's domination of the tied trade has led some critics to suggest that the most important reform to campaign for is the abolition of the system itself. Pub tenants would then be free to serve any beer they liked and drinkers would get a wider choice. Healthy competition would weaken the hold that the Big Six have on the entire trade, not just on the tied houses. In the wake of the Price Commission report in 1977, Labour MP Gwylym Roberts suggested that the Monopolies Commission should outlaw tied houses and added: 'If the tie were removed there would be much healthier competition leading to more choice and a better deal all round for consumers.' The *Daily Mirror* gave the speech front-page banner headlines: 'Brewers face bid to set pubs free: Power to your elbow.'

It seems an exciting idea: no endless rows of Ind Coope pubs in the mid-Chilterns or Courage houses in Avon. Proliferating free houses everywhere, bulging with a wide variety of beers. In fact, it is nonsense and the small brewers, who should stand to gain from such a situation, dread the thought. The people who put forward the idea have no grasp of the power of vast industrial combines, their resilience in adapting to changed situations and their interlocking interests with other parts of society. Tony Ruddle, who runs Ruddles brewery in Leicestershire, is quite clear what the result of breaking the tie would be: 'There are conceivably only two possible alternative owners. First the government - but the amount of cash involved would make it virtually impossible. Secondly there are property groups who do have enormous amounts of money to spend. But these could never be kept separate from the big brewers. If, for example, Watney were forced to sell all their pubs they would be bound to set up separate property companies and keep a substantial stake in them.'

If Britain's tied houses were all put on the market tomorrow, property companies acting for the Big Six would quickly snap them up. Their enormous resources would ensure that they ended up with more pubs than they have now and the independent brewers would be struggling for survival. And even if brewers were not allowed to own pubs there would be a simple way for them to skirt the law. As already happens in the club trade, financial inducements would be offered to landlords if they agreed to take beer only from one company. Pubs would be renovated, with smart new furniture, bar fittings and decorations on the tried and tested principle of commercial back-scratching. F.D. Simpkiss, chairman of the tiny west midlands brewery of the same name, summed up the situation of the small companies when he said: 'We can't possibly compete with the big brewers in anything. We still have a fair amount of club trade but if clubs ever need a loan for improvements we can't possibly supply it and so we lose their business to Mitchells and Butlers or Ansells.'

Some of the regional companies, such as Greenall Whitley or Greene King are substantial enough to survive if the tied system were abolished. But for the vast majority of small brewers, the Simpkisses of this world, disaster would stare them in the face. The accountants and chemists who now dominate the big brewers would be joined by property speculators and together they would wreak even greater havoc on the British pub and its beer.

The Erroll Report on licensing laws suggested in 1972 that restrictions on obtaining a licence should be liberalised, 'the general objective being to permit the sale of alcoholic drinks, for on or off consumption, by any retailers whose character and premises satisfy certain minimum standards. If the tendency would be for the free retail trade to grow in size and strength at the expense of the tied trade, brewers would find themselves competing directly with each other for an increasing proportion of the trade.' Tony Ruddle is an enthusiastic supporter of such reform, which, he feels, would 'encourage the family outlet in the Continental style. I think we have sufficient traditional pubs, but we don't have that type of outlet in this country. There are too many small, poor pubs here. In an ideal situation, in, say a very small village, all the services could be under one roof: post office, cafe, local shop and pub.'

But would such pub-shops sell Tony Ruddle's beer? The Continental experience suggests otherwise. In France, the brewing industry has been monopolised in a sadly similar way to Britain and most of the cafes sell beer from the big combines of Kronenbourg, Kanterbrau, Pelforth and Fischer-Pecheur. This view is upheld by CAMRA's Monopolies Committee. Their secretary, Brian Sheridan, feels that giving licences away would not serve the interests of drinkers, however superficially attractive the Erroll recommendations are. 'It would not produce the desired result,' Sheridan told *What's Brewing* in 1977. 'Freedom of licences would mean lots of cafes selling beer without the facilities for handling cask beer. The big brewers would have a huge advantage, going round promoting their nationally-advertised brands. That is what has happened in France, where

Kronenbourg have just marched across the whole country.'

CAMRA's attitude is that publicans should have a legal right to sell one draught beer from another company. The suggestion has been taken up with some keenness by the National Union of Licensed Victuallers, to the rage of the Brewers' Society. At the end of 1977, NULV spokesmen attacked the society for distributing a secret memorandum to its members recommending that they organise urgent meetings with their tenants to attack the policy for relaxing the tie. The society's fear of greater choice for consumers hardly squares with their fierce championing of 'free competition'.

Another sound suggestion is to ask the government to vary the way in which excise duty is levied, with small brewers paying less than the big ones. That is the legal position in Germany, and the United States followed suit at the end of 1977 when the House of Representatives passed legislation reducing beer duty by two dollars a barrel on the first 60,000 barrels brewed by companies whose annual output is less than two million barrels a year.

Most of the suggestions for relaxing or reforming the tied system founder on the rocks of industrial reality. The Big Six have the financial muscle to brush aside minor tinkering. Britain's pubs and beer will only shake off the big brewers' domination when the combines are broken up in the public interest. If that were done then a radical reorganisation of the way in which beer is sold would be possible, with brewers allowed to own only a small number of tied outlets, or perhaps none at all, and the public house system controlled by local authorities or by specially created public bodies.

Root-and-branch change is vital if a number of small brewers are to survive. The resurgence of real ale by no means guarantees their future, which could disappear as a result of takeover or swingeing death duties. Some people would consider that to be no loss. CAMRA has been attacked from the left, and by the paper *The Leveller* in particular, for propping up small, conservative, even feudal brewing concerns simply because they produce good beer. Some of the criticism is justified. The annual reports from the chairmen of some independent brewing companies make Sir Keith Joseph sound like a dangerous radical.

92

The forelock-tugging, 'morning Mr Cecil, morning Mr Claude' attitudes expected of their staff belong in a museum of antiquated industrial relations. But what would the critics prefer - that the small firms disappear along with the beers and that the monopolisation of the industry be strengthened? Or would they like to see one nationalised brewing concern providing the nation's ale? The prospect of drinking Britfizz produced by a vast state monopoly does not set my heart beating fast with pleasurable excitement. Unlike coal or trains, foodstuffs must retain their regional tastes and characters and any new form of ownership must safeguard the wide varieties of beers still available in Britain.

While the attitudes of the small companies towards their employees leave a lot to be desired, it is the national combines that suffer from almost unending labour disputes. Throughout 1977, all the brewing giants suffered from disputes that in many cases left thousands of pubs without beer for weeks on end. Some company spokesman complained, in the comfortable modern jargon, of 'subversives' and 'militants' leading well-meaning employees astray. The reality is simply that many of the disputes were caused by high-handed management decisions taken often hundreds of miles from the places where they had to be implemented. The workers, in several cases, were openly expressing their anger at the way they felt manipulated by bureaucracies over which they had no control. At least those problems do not occur in small units of production with instant, face-to-face discussions.

Throughout this book, profits have been used as the yardstick of success, or lack of it. It is not, in my view, the only yardstick that can be used, but it is the only one currently available. In any future reorganisation of the industry, social need, and the requirements of drinkers in towns and villages in all parts of the land, should come first. Breaking up the Big Six will be dismissed as a romantic dream. But other systems do exist, or have done so, and the consumers seem well pleased with the result, the beer in their glasses.

The best known system was the late lamented 'nationalised' brewery in Carlisle. The brewery and its pubs were technically owned by the state but were effectively run as a local municipalised concern, though formally under the control of the Home Office. The Carlisle and District State Management Scheme was brought in in 1916. A massive munitions factory had been built at Gretna to fuel the war effort and the government spread alarming stories of the drunkenness and disorder that resulted from the munitions workers' forays into Carlisle, just across the border.

Some historians of the period write that the claims were much exaggerated and were used to pander to the anti-drink attitudes of the Minister of Munitions, Lloyd George. Nevertheless two measures were introduced to tackle the problem. On a national scale, licensing hours were curtailed in order that munitions workers could be kept at their benches; today's pub hours are the result of that wartime legislation. In Carlisle three breweries were closed and production was centred on the fourth, the Carlisle Old Brewery at Caldewgate. The brewery and all the pubs, hotels and off-licences were placed under the rigid control of the Liquor Control Board. Similar schemes were set up in Scotland and in London but did not survive the end of the war. The Carlisle scheme was continued, though. The bureaucratic control of the liquor board was replaced by the state management scheme, which soon acquired a good reputation for its willingness to please local consumers. The range of beer was good, prices were cheap and the 170 pubs were, in general, pleasant places to enjoy a pint or two. By the 1960s, the State Management Scheme (SMS) pubs offered draught bitter and mild in cask, top pressure or keg form; it produced several bottled beers and allowed more than 20 brews from commercial companies to compete with its own products. The consumers could hardly have had a better deal.

The Conservative government that came to power in 1970 quickly put a stop to such nonsense. It said it was undesirable for the state to run a brewery and to own pubs, and added that the SMS had a monopoly of outlets in Carlisle. In an act of blinkered political vandalism, the government smashed the scheme. The pubs were sold off to Greenall Whitley, the biggest independent brewer in the country, to Courage and Scottish and Newcastle. Theakstons of Masham, Yorkshire, bought the brewery and to date have been unable to run it at full capacity. So the appalling monopoly of the SMS was ended, thanks to Greenall Whitley, who have a monopoly of pubs in parts of Cheshire, Courage, who dominate the county of Avon and did so much for choice in the Barnsley area, and S & N who bestride much of Scotland and the north-east. Neither the government nor the brewers consulted the consumers. The fact that they were happy with their pubs and the excellent range of beer was totally irrelevant. The banner of free enterprise had triumphed, borne aloft by Courage and Scottish and Newcastle. It is a banner that bears a close resemblance to the skull and crossbones.

Fortunately other examples of publicly-owned brewing survive. The Northern Federation Clubs is a co-operative that is now one of the major brewers in Britain. It supplies 1,300 clubs, mainly in the north-east but with increasing trade in Yorkshire and the midlands. It has an annual turnover exceeding £10 million and in the first 50 years of its existence it returned more than £18 million in dividends to its affiliated clubs. Its output is more than 300,000 gallons of beer a week.

The Fed, as it is known, was set up in Newcastle-upon-Tyne in 1919. A shortage of beer following the war led the brewers to supply their tied houses first, leaving clubs in the north-east - sports clubs, miners' clubs, working men's clubs, Labour and Tory clubs - to fend for themselves. Some of the clubs got together and toured the mining villages with a horse and cart, asking for investments to buy a brewery at 7½ per cent interest. £10,000 was raised and brewing, after one false start, began in 1921. It is now a massive brewing operation and in 1979 is due to move to bigger premises so that production could be doubled. It produces some of the cheapest and best of the processed 'bright' beers. The Fed is owned by the clubs that it supplies. The stake of each club is determined by the number of barrels it can take a week. Profits are distributed in the form of dividends to the clubs every six weeks and the remaining surplus is ploughed back into the brewery. The Fed is not perfect. It went on the takeover trail itself in the 1970s and swallowed the co-operative Yorkshire Clubs brewery, a small tragedy because Yorkshire Clubs produced excellent cask-conditioned beer.

On the other side of the coin, the Fed gave the South

Wales Clubs Brewery a large, low-interest loan when the Welsh co-operative needed to expand its production facilities. South Wales, now renamed Crown Brewery, remains a flourishing concern owned by the 360 clubs that take its beers, which are supplied in cask form as well as tank. The two co-operatives have been in operation for nearly sixty years and the fact that they have survived and flourished in the era of the national combines is testimony to the fact that the big brewers cannot supply beer of the right quality and price.

The co-operative principle should be expanded. CAMRA has opposed Capital Transfer Tax on the grounds that small, family-owned brewing companies could be forced out of business when the present generation who run the companies die. I share CAMRA's concern to maintain as many brewers as possible, but I think it is wrong to oppose CTT, which has attempted to right a major social injustice, particularly since no CTT is levied if the owners of a company give it to a trust whose beneficiaries are the workers (for example, a workers' cooperative) or if it is made over to a local authority.

When family brewing companies can no longer continue in business because of CTT (and none has yet been forced out of business) then there is a strong case for preserving that company as a vital asset to the community. The brewery and its tied houses could either be taken over by the local authority or, better still, a scheme similar to the Carlisle one could be set up to administer both the brewing of beer and the pubs in which it is served. It could be written into the rules of such a scheme that both brewery-conditioned and cask-conditioned beer should be supplied to the tied houses and that beers from other companies will be allowed to compete with them.

An alternative scheme would be for the tied houses of a company faced by dissolution to band together as a co-operative, raising capital either on the market or, better still, from the government, to keep the brewery in production. The investment level of the pubs would be determined by their weekly barrelage and profits from the brewery would be distributed in the form of dividends. In all of these schemes, pub tenants and managers, brewery workers and consumer representatives should be involved in the running of the publicly-owned or co-operatively owned concerns, marking an important breakthrough for workers' and consumers' control.

But still the major problem remains: what to do with the Big Six. As the Monopoly Commission and the Price Commission have proved, the brewing combines work against the public interest. They are inefficient, their products are generally poor and overpriced and they force them on the consumers through their control of a majority of the tied houses. The case for the break up of the Big Six is unanswerable.

Watney, Truman, Websters, Wilsons, Drybrough and Ushers should be restored as independent companies. Bass Worthington, Mitchells and Butlers, Tennents and Charrington should once again trade separately. Ind Coope, Ansells and Tetley should part company. Courage and John Smith should be prised from the smoky embrace of the Imperial Group and allowed to trade as independent concerns. The Whitbread umbrella should be left in the lost property office and such famous names in brewing as Brickwoods, Strongs, Wethered, Fremlins and Duttons allowed to reappear. Scottish Brewers should be disentangled from Newcastle in an attempt to restore some choice to the parched regions of the North-east and Scotland. No major company should be allowed to have a financial stake exceeding 10 per cent in another firm, so removing the possibility of takeover of such firms as Ruddles, Marstons and Boddingtons. The number of tied houses that any company can own should be strictly limited by law.

If any of the companies liberated in this way could not survive on a commercial basis, then the municipal or co-operative schemes outlined above should be introduced to keep them in operation. Provision would have to be made in any major reorganisation for genuine hardship to shareholders. Although brewing staff should not be affected by such a shake-up, smaller distribution areas could lead to cut-backs in staff. The unions involved would have to ensure that as many workers as possible would be absorbed in other departments and that any inevitable redundancies should be covered by 'natural wastage'.

But does it matter? After all, it's only beer. Ten million pub users think beer is sufficiently important to fork out an average 30p a pint for it every day. Unless the interests of the nation's pub users are taken into account and sweeping changes made in the brewing and supply of beer, then the future is bleak. Small breweries will fall by the wayside, the domination of the Big Six will increase and 'unprofitable' lines such as real draught beer will disappear as beer drinkers are drowned in lager.

More than just real ale will die. Most of the talk about 'Britain's heritage' is jingoistic nonsense that harks back to a Merrie England that was anything but merry for most of its citizens. But our ale and our pubs are different. They offer pleasure to millions. We need our pubs as warm havens in an increasingly harsh world and we need good, traditional beer with a smack of malt and hops to cheer us after the day's work.

They are an important part of a real heritage that is worth fighting to preserve today, for a better tomorrow.

# Appendix:
# The Big Six and their interests

## Bass Charrington

Bass Ltd, Bass Production, Bass Marketing; Bass Ireland; Bass North; Bass North West; Bass South West; Bass Worthington; Charrington and Co; Hewitt Bros; Mitchells and Butlers; Tennent Caledonian; Welsh Brewers; Stones; Bass Charrington Services; Bass Charrington Vintners (including Hedges and Butler); Bass International; Canada Dry; Crest Hotels; Bass Europe (incorporated in the Netherlands); Bass Continental NV (incorporated in the Netherlands); Bass NV (Belgium), including Lamot, Bass Import Bottlers and Crest Hotels); Alexis Lichine et Cie SA (France); Société Viticole de Chateau Lascombes SA (France). 10,000 tied houses in UK.

## Allied Breweries

Allied Breweries (UK) Ltd; Allied Breweries (Production) Ltd; Ansells; Ind Coope; Ind Coope (Scotland); Joshua Tetley; Aylesbury Brewery Co; Showerings, Vine Products and Whiteways; Britvic; Cater, Stoffel & Fortt; Curtis Distillery; Glen Rossie Distillers; Grants of St James; Harveys of Bristol; Hatch, Mansfield and Co; John Harvey & Sons; John Harvey and Sons (Espana); Minster (Soft Drinks); J.R. Phillips; Samuel Dow; Showerings Ltd; Stewart and Son; Teachers Distillers; Victoria Wine Co; Vine Products; Whiteways; William Gaymer; Wine Market; Woolley, Duval & Beaufoys; A Delor & Cie SA (France); Cantrell & Cochrane Ireland (50 per cent); Cockburn Smithes & Cia (Portugal); Allied International; Allied Breweries (Australia); Looza SA (Brussels); Allied

Investments (Bermuda); Skol International Investments (Bermuda); Skol International Ltd (Bermuda); Ind Coope African Investments Ltd; Skol Browerijen NV (Netherlands); Erven Warnink BV (Netherlands). 7,600 tied houses in UK.

## Courage

Courage is a subsidiary of Imperial Group and includes John Smith of Tadcaster and Newark. Courage Eastern; Courage Central; Courage Western; Saccone and Speed, Arthur Cooper (Wine Merchants); Saccone and Speed International; Anchor Hotels and Taverns; Harp Lager (third share); Taunton Cider (third share); Cantrell & Cochrane UK (27.5 per cent share); Courage Australia (41.9 per cent); Saccone and Speed (Gibraltar); Saccone and Speed (Malta); Saccone and Speed (Spain); Saccone and Speed (USA); El Alcasar SA Spain (10 per cent); John Smith SA Belgium; Simonds-Farsons-Cisk Malta (26.3 per cent): 5,800 tied houses in UK.

## Watney Mann & Truman

Part of the Grand Metropolitan Group. Berni Inns; Schooner Inns; Truman Taverns; Watney Innkeepers; Watney Taverns, Carbery Milk Products; Express Dairy Foods; Fromageries Lutin; Virginia Milk Products; Woodhouse Hume; Express Dairies (London, Northern and Western); Hawley's Bakeries; Hunt's Dairies; Independent Bakeries; Marshalls Dairies; North Devon Eggs; Primrose and Len Dairies; Scottish Farmers Dairy Co; Sloans Dairies; Tavistock Services; Periton Travel Services; Utell International; Croft; IDV Europe; IDV Home Trade; IDV Export; Justerini and Brooks; Gilbey Vintners; Morgan Furze; Peter Dominic; Westminster Wine; Gilbeys Australia; Gilbey Canada; Gilbey France; Croft Portugal, Croft Jerez Spain; W & A Gilbey South Africa; Watney Mann; Truman; Coca-Cola Southern Bottlers, Drybrough; Samuel Webster; Watney International; Cantrell & Cochrane UK (72.5 per cent). 7,000 tied houses in UK.

## Whitbread

Whitbread East Pennines; Whitbread Flowers; Whitbread Fremlins; Whitbread London; Whitbread Scotland; Whitbread

Wales; Whitbread Wessex; Whitbread West Pennines; Thomas Wethered & Sons; Whitbread International; Stowells of Chelsea; Thresher & Co; Langenbach GmbH (West Germany); R. White & Sons; Long John International; Railway Tavern Ltd; Whitbread Investment; Whitbread Trafalgar Properties (49 per cent); Whitly Inns. 7,000 tied houses in the UK.

## Scottish and Newcastle

Scottish and Newcastle Breweries; Thistle Hotels; Brewers Food Supply Co; Glenallachie Distillery; Isle of Jura Distillery; Waverley Vintners; Canongate Wines; Christopher & Co; Welcome Inns; Scottish and Newcastle Importers (USA); SARL Baleyre (France); SCI Le Halèvy (France); Golf St Cyprien SA (France); Highland Tourist (third share); Del Monte (Kitchens) Ltd (49 per cent); Harp Lager (one third share); Harp Ship Stores Ltd (20 per cent); High Gosforth Park Co (10 per cent). 1,100 tied houses in UK.

## Sources and further reading

Monopolies Commission. *Report on the Supply of Beer*, HMSO 1969.

*Report of the Departmental Committee on Liquor Licensing*, HMSO 1972. Cmnd 5154. Chairman, Lord Erroll of Hale.

Price Commission. *Beer Prices and Margins*, 1977. Report No. 31.

Ministry of Agriculture. Food Standards Committee. *Report on Beer*, 1977.

Frank Baillie, *The Beer Drinker's Companion*, Newton Abbot, David & Charles, 1973.

Richard Boston, *Beer and Skittles*, London, Collins, 1976 and Fontana, 1977.

Michael Hardman and Theo Bergstrom, *Beer Naturally*, London, Bergstrom & Boyle, 1976.

John Hunt, *A City under the Influence (The Carlisle State Management Scheme)*, Carlisle, Lakescene Publications, 1971.

Christopher Hutt, *Death of the English Pub*, London, 1973.

*The Brewer; Brewer's Guardian; Brewer's Review; What's Brewing*

## Organisations for further information

National Union of Licensed Victuallers, Downing Street, Farnham, Surrey, to which local Licensed Victuallers Associations are affiliated - the organisation of public house tenants.

National Association of Licensed House Managers, 9 Coombe Lane, London SW20, a trade union affiliated to the TUC - the organisation of public house managers.

Campaign for Real Ale Ltd, 34 Alma Road, St Albans, Herts, an organisation representing drinkers of traditional beer. Membership of CAMRA is £4 a year. It produces a monthly newspaper, *What's Brewing*, and the annual *Good Beer Guide* (£1.95) which lists 5,000 of the best real ale pubs in the UK and the original gravities of all draught beers. CAMRA branches produce their own county guides.

Most brewery workers are members of the Transport and General Workers Union. A few pub managers and brewery clerical staff belong to the TGWU's clerical section. Most bar staff are unorganised and work long hours for low wages.

# Beer Drinkers' Handbook

*The history of beer has been traced back to 4000 BC in Mesopotamia, when malted barley was allowed to ferment with the natural yeasts in the air. This type of fermented drink, almost certainly sweet and syrupy in taste, spread through the Middle East to western Europe before the Christian era. Barley was grown in Britain before Christian times and a fermented drink that became known as ale became popular and widespread throughout the British Isles.*

Until the fourteenth century British ale was brewed without hops, though herbs were added as preservatives. Hops were introduced to Britain by Dutch brewers and for a time a major controversy raged over the merits of hopless ale and hopped bier or beer. But eventually all British-brewed beers used hops and the names ale and beer are now synonymous.

Today all beer in Britain is brewed in the same, traditional way, though unnatural ingredients are often used and are dealt with in the chapter 'Nasty Bits' in the main body of the book.

Beer begins, as it has always done, with barley, a cereal that is rich in natural sugars. Barley grown for brewing comes from East Anglia, Scotland, the Midlands, Hampshire, Oxfordshire and Berkshire. It should have a high starch content and low nitrogen level.

When the barley has been harvested it is taken to maltings where the barley grains are soaked in water. The barley starts to germinate and the grains are then taken to a germination area where the grains continue to grow for up to eight days. Germination helps convert the starch content of the grains into natural sugars.

The grains are transferred to a kiln room where they are heated to about 60°C (140°F), which stops the germination. The temperature is then raised, according to the type of beer required. The temperature is kept quite low if a pale malt is required. Extra kilning at much higher

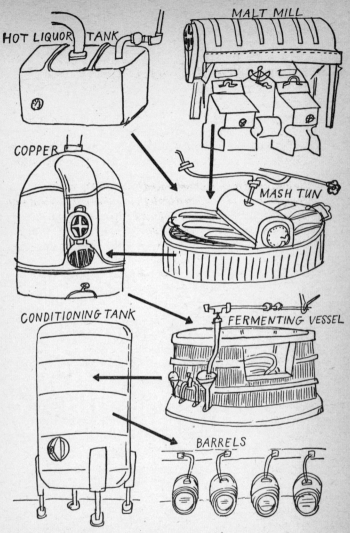

HOT LIQUOR TANK

MALT MILL

COPPER

MASH TUN

CONDITIONING TANK

FERMENTING VESSEL

BARRELS

temperatures is needed to produce dark malts for beers like Guinness stout.

Some breweries have their own maltings but the process is usually carried out by specialist maltsters. The malted barley is then taken to the brewery where it is ground in a mill to a fine powder called grist. The grist is poured into a vessel called a mash tun and is mixed or 'mashed' with hot water. Water is always called liquor by brewers and is kept in special liquor tanks. Most breweries have their own wells but they supplement the well water with water from the public supply. The water is specially treated to ensure purity. Many brewers attempt to reproduce water similar to the type found at Burton-upon-Trent, a famous brewing centre where the natural well waters are ideal for light bitter beers. London water used to be more suitable for darker beers but is now treated according to the type of beer required.

The thick, porridgy liquid in the mash tun stands for several hours while the sugars in the malt dissolve into the liquor. The liquid is then run off and the malt grains left behind are sprayed with more hot liquor to make sure that no valuable sugars are left behind. This is known as 'sparging'. The spent grains are sold off as animal feedstuffs, often called brewers' grains.

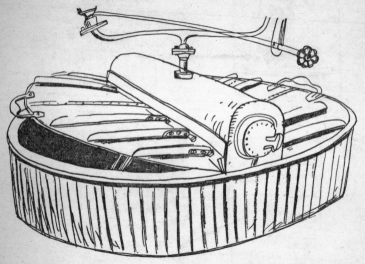

The sweet liquid from the mash tun is called wort, pronounced 'wert'. It is run into a copper where it is boiled with hops. Hops are a climbing plant with names such as Goldings, Fuggles and Northern Brewer and are grown in Kent, Sussex, Hampshire, Hereford and Worcester. Hops give beer bitterness and aroma and act as a preservative. They are picked in the autumn, the cones separated from the leaves and stalks and then taken to oast houses with their familiar cowls, where they are heated and dried and either sent to the breweries as dry hops or compressed into 'hop pellets'. The wort in the copper is boiled for about two hours and acids from the hops dissolve into the liquid.

Boiling kills off any bacteria in the wort. In some breweries,

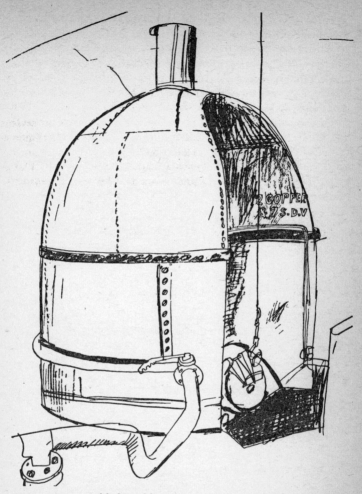

extra sugars are added at this stage, according to the recipe. After boiling the wort is run into a vessel called a hop back, which has a slotted base. The hops settle on the base and act as a filter as the wort runs through. The spent hops are then collected and sold as fertiliser.

The wort is cooled and is run into fermentation vessels ready for the vital process that will turn it into fermented alcohol. Before yeast is added, an Excise officer will take a sample of the liquid to determine its original gravity, the measure of fermentable materials added to water. Brewers pay duty according to the gravity of the liquid: the higher the gravity - that is, the greater the proportion of fermentable materials -

the greater the duty. Then the yeast is added or 'pitched' and thoroughly mixed with the wort. Yeast consists of fungus cells that grow by germinating with sweet liquids. In order to ensure strict quality of beer, special strains of yeast have been developed and breweries are kept scrupulously clean to avoid wild strains of yeast affecting the brew. Some yeasts are used over and over again: the yeasts developed by Bass in Burton for beers such as draught Bass have been used for more than 150 years and are likely to go on multiplying for that amount of time again.

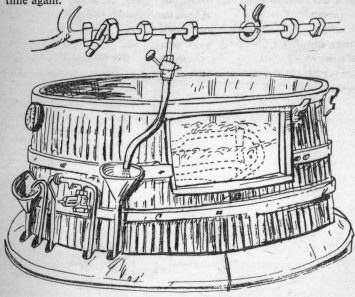

The yeast converts the sugars in the wort into alcohol. About twelve hours after the yeast is pitched the carbon dioxide gas given off by the fermentation creates a thick head on the liquid. The head is skimmed off; some is kept for future use, the rest is sold as yeast extract, the best-known brand being Marmite. As the sugars in the brew are used up the yeast slowly sinks to the bottom of the fermentation vessel. After about five days, fermentation is complete.

The fermented liquid, often called 'green beer', is run into conditioning tanks where the remaining yeast continues to convert sugar into alcohol and carbon dioxide. Finings, made from the swim bladders of fish, are added to drag the yeast to the bottom of the tank. Priming sugar is sometimes added to encourage a secondary fermentation. The beer is then run into casks. Some breweries add dry hops to improve the aroma.

The beer is ready for delivery to the pubs. It is transported on lorries known as brewers' drays. Most are motorised but a number of brewers, large and small, still use horse-drawn drays for short journeys in town and country. At the pub, the casks of beers are either set up in the bar or, more usually these days, rolled down into deep, cool cellars where the beer should be kept at a constant temperature of about 13°C (55°F). Casks can be made from either wood or metal and some are lined with nylon or plastic. Ranging from 4½ gallons to 54 gallons, they have intriguing old names such as pin, firkin, kilderkin, barrel and hogshead. It is wrong to use the term barrel for all sizes of cask as this denotes a special size - 36 gallons. Some brewers now use metric-sized casks and others use specially-converted kegs. This is the case with Watney Mann & Truman, who phased out all cask beers and had to use converted kegs when demand forced them to brew traditional beer again.

The casks need to stand for up to 48 hours while the sediment of yeast and hops settles to the bottom. The casks are laid on their sides and held by a cradle or by chocks. A cask has two holes: a large bung hole to serve the beer and a smaller hole on top, the shive hole, which allows natural carbon dioxide to escape. A wooden peg, called a spile, is knocked into the shive hole.

The beer undergoes its vital secondary fermentation. The carbon dioxide produced escapes through the spile while the beer gains in maturity and flavour. When the beer has stopped 'working', that is, fermenting vigorously, the soft spile or peg is replaced by a hard spile, which controls the escape of gas more rigidly and helps keep the beer in condition. But as air has replaced the CO2, the beer will stay in good condition for only a few days.

To stop air getting to the beer, some publicans are encouraged by their breweries to connect a cylinder of carbon dioxide to the spile hole. In some cases the gas pressure is kept low and is known as blanket pressure. In other cases, the pressure is increased so that it forces the beer to the bar. This is known as top pressure. These methods stop the beer maturing properly and the CO2 dissolved in the beer makes it fizzy like a processed, artificially carbonated beer.

Most beer does not reach the pub cellar in its traditional form. To avoid the problem of natural beer going out of condition, brewers developed 'bright' beer. This is chilled and filtered in the brewery to remove any yeast and other solids. This type of beer does not need time to settle before being served and needs little care and attention. It cannot undergo a secondary fermentation and therefore even the best bright beers, such as those brewed for the club trade, lack the full maturity and flavour of traditional beer. Bright beer is taken to pubs or clubs in large tankers, where it is pumped into large cellar tanks and kept under gas pressure.

The ultimate in unnatural, processed beer is keg. It is a sterile brew that will last for up to three months. It is chilled and filtered in the brewery and usually pasteurised to make sure that no life remains. It is put into sealed containers called kegs, which have just one opening to serve the beer, and the remaining space is filled with carbon dioxide. The gas is used to serve the beer, to give it some fake life and sparkle and to hide the fact that it has little or no flavour.

In the pub cellar, the kegs are connected to cylinders of $CO_2$, although some kegs are so heavily impregnated with gas in the brewery that no extra $CO_2$ is necessary: when the tap in the bar is opened, the keg acts like an aerosol and the beer is pushed to the service point. When a cylinder is connected to the keg, the gas pushes the beer to the bar in the same way.

Traditional beer is served in England and Wales straight from the cask, by a beer engine or by an electric pump. When the beer comes straight from the cask it is known as 'gravity dispense'. A tap is hammered into the bung hole and the beer flows into the glass when the tap is opened. This method is still quite common in rural pubs that do not have cellars and many town pubs have small casks of winter ale on their bars in the winter. The advantage of the method is that the beer does not have to travel through yards of piping that must be kept scrupulously clean to avoid infection. The disadvantage is that the beer can become warm if it is kept in the bar.

A beer engine is recognised by the handpumps on the bar, the tall truncheon-like levers that operate a simple suction pump when pulled back. The pump or engine draws the beer from the cask in the cellar through the pipes and into the glass. One pull on the pump delivers about half a pint. The term 'draught beer' derives from the fact that the beer is drawn from the cask. Processed beer that is pushed to the bar by gas pressure does not deserve the name draught. Although handpumps in a pub are usually the sign of real beer, there are fake pumps that operate a lever when pulled and processed beer is delivered.

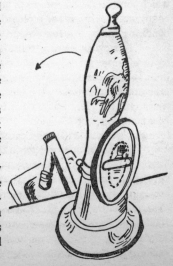

Electric pumps do exactly the same job as a beer engine but without the effort. When the tap is opened on the bar, an electric pump

in the cellar is operated and draws the beer from the cask to the bar. Some electric pumps are known as diaphragm dispensers: a diaphragm moves to and fro inside the dispense box on the bar, metering exact half pints or full pints into the glass. Another form of electric pump is the free-flow pump: when the tap is opened the beer flows into the glass until the tap is closed.

In Scotland the traditional method of dispense for draught beer is the water engine, recognised by tall fonts or pillars on the bar. The water engine converts mains water pressure into air pressure which pushes the beer to the bar. Many water engines are being replaced by electric air compressors that do exactly the same job. There is a limited amount of air pressure dispense south of the border. Some Charrington pubs in the Greater London area use air pressure to serve draught beer and some Watney and Truman pubs use a new method of air pressure dispense developed by the Distillers Company.

Keg beers are served by pressure taps. The problem with this method is that it is sometimes hard to distinguish a pressure tap from an electric pump but usually the pressure method has a more elaborate bar mounting advertising one of the national keg beers. When the tap is opened the pressurised beer is pushed to the bar under heavy $CO_2$ pressure.

Most bottled beers are like keg beer. They are chilled, filtered and pasteurised in the brewery and bottled with added carbon dioxide. But if you find yourself in a pub that offers nothing but processed 'draught' beers there is usually the saving grace of bottled Guinness. This is a naturally-conditioned bottled beer that is allowed to mature in the bottle. It has a sediment of yeast in the bottom and if you don't fancy drinking that you can pour the beer slowly and carefully to leave the last few drops in the bottle. But the yeast will do you no harm. A good publican will carefully note the delivery dates of his bottled Guinness, giving the beer time to reach its best condition before serving.

Another nationally available naturally-conditioned bottled beer is White Shield Worthington, brewed by Bass. This is a strong pale ale with a delightful nutty flavour. Because it is lighter than Guinness it is possible to see the sediment in the glass and great care and skill in pouring is practised by White Shield devotees to keep the yeast from entering the glass - although other equally dedicated drinkers feel that the yeast should be drunk as well. White Shield is in drinkable condition about four weeks after being bottled and will stay in good condition for about nine months.

Some Courage pubs sell a naturally-conditioned beer called Russian Imperial Stout and a few independent brewers produce fine bottled beers: Eldridge Pope's Thomas Hardy Ale, Gale's Prize Old Ale, Traquair House in Scotland (some of this is pasteurised), Brahms and Liszt Special Pale Ale from the Selby brewery, Own Ale from the Miners Arms in Somerset and John Boothroyd's York Brewery Extra Strong.

Unlike bottled Guinness, 'draught' Guinness is a processed beer, though of a much higher quality than most keg beers. In Britain, the beer is pasteurised and is served by a mixture of carbon dioxide and nitrogen, which makes the beer smoother and less gassy than other kegs. The gas is kept in a separate compartment inside the keg and therefore does not dissolve into the beer in the same manner as other kegs. In Ireland the beer is not pasteurised and is a fine-tasting beer even though served by gas pressure.

Many brewers produce two bitters, a best bitter and a weaker ordinary bitter. If they bottle these beers they will usually call them pale ale after the best bitter and light ale to denote the ordinary. A number of brewers produce a draught bitter called IPA. This is short for India Pale Ale and derives from a beer of exceptional quality brewed by Bass for the East India Company. A number of beers still have an X in their name, such as Wadworth's 6X. This comes from the medieval habit of marking casks with Xs to denote the strength. In Scotland many beers are still called '60 shilling' or '80 shilling' after an old form of excise duty levied on the strength of the beer.

Just as pale or light ales are bottled versions of draught bitter, so brown ale is the bottled form of mild beer. Mild is normally weaker in strength than bitter and darker in colour, though a number of breweries brew light milds that are more like weak bitters. Mild is declining in most parts of the country, which is a pity as there are many excellent mild ales that are a sensible drink for a lunchtime or long 'session'. Many brewers also produce strong barley wine type beers called old ales or winter warmers.

In Scotland bitter is rarely called by that name. Ordinary bitter is called 'heavy' and best bitter is often called 'export', while mild, even though dark in colour, is known as 'light'. In the north-east, export also means a strong bitter while ordinary bitter is often known as 'Scotch'.

The strength of beer is measured for excise purposes in the fermentation tank prior to the yeast being pitched. A measure is taken of the original gravity of the wort, that is the amount of fermentable material added to the water. Water has a gravity of 1000 degrees, so a beer with an OG of 1036 will have had 36 parts of fermentable material added to the water. When the beer has finished fermentation the final gravity, specific gravity, will be considerably lower than the OG, but knowing the OG will give a reasonable indication of the strength of the beer you are drinking. Most brewers now disclose the OG of their beers but as yet there is no legislation requiring this information to be given in pubs.

Another method of expressing the strength of a beer is by the percentage of alcohol in the liquid. This requires a rather complicated sum based on the OG and SG of the beer but a rough but fairly accurate way of determining the percentage of alcohol is to take the known OG of a beer - say 1036 - delete the first two figures and place a decimal point between the remaining ones, i.e. 3.6 per cent alcohol. Strong beer is not better than weak beer and there is no merit in drinking several pints of strong beer to prove 'manliness'. Beer should be drunk for enjoyment and there are many excellent milds and weak bitters that are better tasting than some high gravity beers, which tend to be rather sweet and cloying in taste.

All beer should be treated with caution. It is an alcoholic drink. It should be drunk because it tastes good and is refreshing, not to get drunk, when you become a nuisance to yourself and other people and a menace on the road. One per cent of the population has a serious drink problem. Drinking is a pleasant, social activity but self-control is needed to keep it within sensible bounds. Within moderation, beer will do you no harm and is mildly beneficial: it is brewed from barley, hops and pure water. As beer is mainly water it is certainly less harmful than spirits or wine.

# A list of breweries and their beers

In this section I use *cask* to indicate real, draught beer allowed to mature in the pub cellar. *Keg* indicates dead, processed, 'brewery-conditioned' beer. Since *all* keg is served under pressure, I reserve *top pressure* to indicate cask beer served under pressure. Some breweries produce both *keg* and *top pressure*.

**Adnams:** Southwold, Suffolk. Bitter, mild and old ale in winter. 72 tied houses, all cask.

**All Nations:** Coalport Road, Madeley, Salop. A home brew pub-cum-brewery, producing just one mild beer, available only at the All Nations. Cask.

**Ansells:** Aston Cross, Birmingham. A subsidiary of Allied Breweries. Mild and bitter. 2,400 tied houses. Mainly top pressure and keg, some cask.

**Arkell:** Kingsdown Brewery, Upper Stratton, Swindon, Wilts. Two bitters and a strong ale. 64 tied houses, about a third selling cask.

**Banks:** Part of Wolverhampton and Dudley Breweries, Park Brewery, Wolverhampton, West Midlands. Mild and bitter. 770 tied houses, most selling cask.

**Bass Charrington:** breweries at Runcorn, Tadcaster, Burton, Belfast, Sheffield, Birmingham, Glasgow and Edinburgh. A vast range of beers, nearly all keg and top pressure but still brewing some excellent cask beers, including draught Bass, Worthington best bitter, Joules bitter and light mild at Burton, plus the bottled Worthington White Shield; Brew Ten, Extra Light and mild at Tadcaster. See also Charrington, Mitchells and Butlers, Welsh and Stones. The group has more than 1000 tied houses.

**Bateman:** Wainfleet, Lincolnshire. Two bitters and a mild. Nearly all the 110 tied houses serve cask.

**Batham:** Brierley Hill, West Midlands. Mild and bitter. Eight tied houses, all with cask.

**Beard:** Lewes, Sussex. Beer brewed for them by Harvey. Half the 26 tied houses serve cask.

114

**Belhaven:** Dunbar, Lothian. Two bitters, a mild and a strong ale. 10 out of 25 tied houses serve cask and about 100 free trade outlets sell the cask.

**Blackawton:** Totnes, Devon. One bitter. No tied houses but serves cask beer to a few pubs and clubs.

 **Blue Anchor:** Helston, Cornwall. A home-brew pub with three cask bitters available only at the Blue Anchor.

 **Boddingtons:** Strangeways Brewery, Manchester. One bitter, two milds and a strong ale. 270 tied houses, all with cask.

**Border:** Wrexham, Clwyd. One bitter and two milds. 200 tied houses, a quarter with cask.

 **Brain:** Cardiff. Two bitters and a mild. More than 100 tied houses, all with cask.

**Brakspear** (Henley Brewery Co): Henley on Thames, Oxon. Two bitters, a mild and an old ale. 130 tied houses, almost all with cask.

 **Matthew Brown** (Lion Ales): Blackburn, Lancs. Mild and bitter. 600 tied houses, a few with cask.

 **Buckley:** Llanelli, Dyfed. Two bitters and a mild. 180 tied houses, about half with cask.

**Burt:** Ventnor, Isle of Wight. Two bitters and a mild. 11 tied houses, some with cask.

 **Burtonwood:** Warrington, Cheshire. One bitter and two milds. 300 tied houses, most with cask.

**Cameron:** Hartlepool, Co Durham. Owned by Ellerman Shipping Lines. Two bitters and a mild. 700 tied houses, many with cask.

**Carlsberg:** Northampton. Keg lager only. No pubs.

**Castletown:** Isle of Man. Mild and bitter. 36 tied houses, only one does not serve cask.

**Charrington:** Mile End, London E1. Subsidiary of Bass Charrington. Two bitters, brewed in Birmingham by Mitchells and Butlers. Most Charrington pubs serve top pressure and keg.

 **Courage:** Breweries at London, Reading, Plymouth and Bristol. 5,800 tied houses, most with only top pressure and keg but the group does produce small amounts of cask mild and bitter at its four breweries, including the famous Directors Bitter from London and Bristol. See also John Smith.

 **Crown:** Pontyclun, Mid-Glamorgan. Formerly the South Wales Clubs Brewery. A cooperative brewery with two bitters for clubs and a few pubs. About 100 of 350 clubs serve cask.

 **Darley:** Doncaster, S Yorks. Bitter and two milds. 88 tied houses, 60 with cask.

**Davenports:** Birmingham. Mild and bitter. 118 tied houses, 50 with cask.

 **Devenish:** Redruth, Cornwall, and Weymouth, Dorset. Cornwall brews two bitters and a mild but serves them under top pressure in most of the 200 tied houses. Weymouth brews mild and bitter and 53 of the 190 pubs serve cask.

 **Donnington:** Stow-on-the-Wold, Glos. Two bitters and a mild. 17 pubs, most with top pressure.

**Drybrough:** Edinburgh. Subsidiary of Watney, Mann and Truman. No cask.

**Eldridge Pope** (Dorchester Brewery): Dorchester, Dorset.

Three bitters and the bottled Thomas Hardy Ale. 180 tied houses, about 50 with cask.

 **Elgood:** Wisbech, Cambs. Mild and bitter. Nearly half the 58 tied houses serve cask.

**Everards:** Leicester. Three bitters and a mild. 134 tied houses, only a few serving cask, but number growing.

**Felinfoel:** Llanelli, Dyfed. Two bitters and a mild. 80 tied houses, most using top pressure, though cask is increasingly available in the free trade.

**Fighting Cocks:** Home brew, Corby Glen, Grantham, Lincs. Pressurised beer available only at the pub. Bought by Melbourns of Stamford in December 1977.

 **Fuller, Smith and Turner:** Chiswick, London W4. Two bitters and a mild. 110 tied houses, 31 with cask.

 **Gale:** Horndean, Hants. Two bitters, two milds, an old ale and the bottled Prize Old Ale. 99 of the 102 tied houses serve cask.

**Gibbs Mew:** Salisbury, Wilts. Bitter and a strong ale. 55 tied houses, a few with cask.

116

**Godson:** Lower Clapton, London E5. One cask bitter, brewed for the free trade. No tied houses.

 **Greenall Whitley:** Breweries at Warrington and Wem. Mild and bitter from Warrington, two bitters and a mild from Wem in Salop. Nearly 1,700 pubs, most with cask. The biggest independent brewers.

 **Greene King** (Abbot): Bury St Edmunds, Suffolk, and Biggleswade, Beds. Two bitters and a mild from Bury, two bitters and two milds from Biggleswade. 850 tied houses, 70 per cent using top pressure.

 **Guernsey** (Pony Ales): St Peter Port, CI. Mild and bitter. 13 of the 50 tied houses serve cask.

**Guinness:** Park Royal, London NW10. Bottled stout and keg stout. No tied houses.

 **Hall and Woodhouse** (Badger Beer): Blandford Forum, Dorset. Two bitters. 162 tied houses, nearly half with cask.

 **Hansons:** Part of Wolverhampton and Dudley Breweries, Dudley, West Midlands. Mild and bitter. See Banks.

 **Hardys and Hansons** (Kimberley Ales): Nottingham. Mild and bitter. 200 tied houses, 170 with cask.

**Harp:** Breweries in Manchester, Edinburgh and Hampshire. Owned by Guinness, Courage, Scottish and Newcastle and Greene King. All keg. No tied houses.

 **Hartleys:** Ulverston, Cumbria. Two bitters and a mild. 58 tied houses, all with cask.

**Harvey:** Lewes, Sussex. Two bitters, a mild and an old ale. Half the 24 tied houses sell cask. Also brews for Beard.

 **Higsons:** Liverpool. Mild and bitter. 100 of the 158 tied houses serve cask.

**Holden:** Dudley, West Midlands. Two bitters, a mild and an old ale. 10 tied houses, most with cask.

**Holt:** Cheetham, Manchester. Mild and bitter. 80 pubs, all with cask.

 **Home:** Daybrook, Nottinghamshire. Mild and bitter. 380 of the 400 tied houses serve cask.

**Hook Norton:** Banbury, Oxon. Mild, bitter and old ale. 34 tied houses, all with cask.

 **Hoskins:** Leicester. Mild, bitter and old ale. One tied house and an off-licence, both with cask.

 **Hull:** North Country Breweries, owned by Northern Foods. Mild and bitter. 210 tied houses, most with cask.

**Hydes:** Manchester. Bitter, two milds and an old ale. 50 tied houses, all with cask.

 **Ind Coope:** Subsidiary of Allied Breweries. Breweries at Romford and Burton. Mild and bitter at Romford, two bitters from Burton. 850 tied houses serve cask.

 **Jennings:** Cockermouth, Cumbria. Mild and bitter. 88 of the 90 tied houses have cask.

**King and Barnes:** Horsham, Sussex. Mild, bitter and old ale. 55 of the 59 tied houses serve cask.

**Lees:** Manchester. Bitter, two milds and an old ale. 150 tied houses, most with cask.

**Litchborough:** Litchborough, Northants. No tied houses. One bitter, mainly top pressure.

**Lorimer:** Edinburgh. A subsidiary of Vaux. One bitter. 205 tied houses, 30 with cask. Lorimer's cask is also sold in a number of Vaux houses.

 **McEwans:** Edinburgh. A subsidiary of Scottish and Newcastle. Two bitters, hard to find in cask form.

**Maclay:** Alloa, Central Scotland. Two bitters and a mild. 25 tied houses, 17 with cask.

 **McMullen:** Hertford. Mild and bitter. 170 tied houses, about half with cask.

**Mansfield:** Mansfield, Notts. No cask.

**Marston, Thompson and Evershed:** Burton-upon-Trent, Staffs. Two bitters, two milds and an old ale. 500 of the 600 tied houses serve cask.

**Mason Arms:** Home brew, Southleigh Witney, Oxon. Cask bitter, available only at the pub.

**Melbourns:** Stamford, Lincs. No longer brewing but supplies Sam Smith's beer to 32 tied houses.

**Miners Arms:** Home brew, Priddy, Somerset. Bottled Own Ale available only with meals in the restaurant at the pub.

**Mitchells:** Lancaster. Two bitters and a mild. 47 tied houses, 45 with cask.

 **Mitchells and Butlers:** A subsidiary of Bass Charrington. Breweries in Birmingham, Walsall and Wolverhampton. Birmingham brews two bitters and a mild, Walsall one mild, and Wolverhampton one bitter. More than 2,000 tied houses, many with cask.

**Morland:** Abingdon, Oxon. Two bitters and a mild. More than half the 220 tied houses serve cask.

 **Morrell:** Oxford. Two bitters, two milds, an old ale and a strong occasional special brew. 140 pubs, only a few with cask.

**Newcastle:** Scottish and Newcastle's Tyneside brewery. All the beer is pressurised but some of the 712 pubs serve McEwans bitter or 80 shilling from Edinburgh in cask form.

**Northern Clubs:** Newcastle-upon-Tyne. Co-operative brewery supplying clubs. Pressurised beer but of an exceptional quality.

 **Okell:** Douglas, Isle of Man. Mild and bitter. 70 tied houses, all with cask.

**Oldham:** Oldham, Greater Manchester. Mild and bitter. 100 tied houses, a quarter with cask.

**Old Swan:** Netherton, Dudley, West Midlands. Home brew pub brewing one cask bitter.

 **Paine:** St Neots, Cambs. Two bitters and a mild. Half the 24 tied houses sell cask.

**Palmer:** Bridport, Dorset. Two bitters. Most pubs sell top pressure beer.

**Penrhos:** Penrhos Court, Kington, Herefordshire. Two cask bitters, brewed for restaurant and local free trade.

 **Pollard:** Stockport, Greater Manchester. One cask bitter. No houses and brews for the free trade.

**Randall:** St. Helier, Jersey. No cask.

 **Randall:** St Peter Port, Guernsey CI. Mild and bitter. Most of the 18 tied houses serve cask.

**Rayment:** Furneux Pelham, Herts. Mild and bitter. A subsidiary of Greene King. Nearly half the 25 tied houses serve cask.

 **Ridley:** Chelmsford, Essex. Mild and bitter. Only one of the 65 tied houses does not serve cask.

**Robinson:** Stockport, Greater Manchester. Two bitters, a mild and an old ale. 318 tied houses - only one without cask.

 **Ruddle:** Oakham, Leics. Two bitters. 36 tied houses, 32 with cask. Cask beers widely available in free trade.

**St Austell:** St Austell, Cornwall. Two bitters and a mild. 132 tied houses, about 80 with cask.

 **Selby:** Selby, North Yorks. Cask bitter, old ale and the bottled Brahms and Liszt Special Pale Ale. Only one tied house.

**Shepherd Neame:** Faversham, Kent. Bitter, mild and old ale. 234 tied houses and all but ten serve cask.

**Shipstone:** New Basford, Nottingham. Mild and bitter. 250 tied houses, nearly all with cask.

 **Simpkiss:** Brierley Hill, West Midlands. Mild, bitter and old ale. 16 tied houses and all but one serve cask.

**Skol:** Breweries in Alloa and Wrexham. Owned by Allied Breweries. No tied houses. All keg lager.

**Smiles:** Colston Yard, Bristol. One cask bitter originally brewed for a restaurant, now available in the free trade.

**John Smith:** A subsidiary of Courage. 1,600 tied houses. No cask.

**Samuel Smith:** Tadcaster, North Yorks. One bitter. More than 300 tied houses, most with cask. Widely available in the free trade.

**Stones:** Sheffield. A subsidiary of Bass Charrington. One bitter. Most of the tied houses serve cask.

 **Taylor:** Keighley, West Yorks. Three bitters, two milds and an old ale. 28 tied pubs, all with cask.

**Tennent:** Glasgow and Edinburgh. A subsidiary of Bass Charrington. Mainly pressurised beer but one cask bitter is brewed in Edinburgh for a few pubs.

**Tetley:** A subsidiary of Allied Breweries. Two breweries in Leeds and Warrington. Leeds produces mild and bitter, Warrington two bitters and a mild. Many of the tied houses serve cask.

**Theakston:** Masham, North Yorks and Carlisle, Cumbria. Brews one bitter, two milds and an old ale, Old Peculier. Only six tied houses, all with cask, but widely available in the free trade. The Carlisle brewery is the former nationalised State Management Scheme brewery.

**John Thompson:** home brew, Ingleby, Derbyshire. One cask bitter, available only at the John Thompson Inn.

**Three Tuns:** Bishops Castle, Salop. Home brew. Cask mild and bitter available at the Three Tuns and one other pub.

**Thwaites:** Blackburn, Lancashire. Bitter and two milds. 380 tied houses, all but 20 serving cask.

**Tolly Cobbold:** Ipswich, Suffolk, a subsidiary of Ellerman Shipping Lines. Two bitters, a mild and an old ale. Nearly half the 360 tied houses serve cask.

**Traquair House:** Innerleithen, Borders. Scotland's only licensed stately home. The bottled beer is usually pasteurised but can be bought in its natural state at the house.

**Truman:** London, E1. A subsidiary of Watney Mann & Truman. Many keg beers, one cask bitter available in 106 of the 900 tied houses.

**Usher:** Trowbridge, Wilts. A subsidiary of Watney Mann & Truman. Two bitters and an old ale. Nearly half the 688 tied houses serve cask.

**Vaux:** Sunderland. Two bitters and a mild. 510 tied houses, 79 with cask.

**Wadworth:** Devizes, Wilts. Two bitters, a light mild and an old ale. 129 of the 143 tied houses serve cask.

**Ward:** A subsidiary of Vaux in Sheffield. Mild and bitter. 96 tied houses, 64 with cask.

**Watney:** part of the Watney Mann & Truman brewing division of Grand Metropolitan. Breweries in London and Norwich and many depots. Only one real beer from London but the Norwich brewery brews four cask beers for London, the South and the Midlands and one for Norfolk. The group has more than 7,000 tied houses.

 **Webster:** Halifax, West Yorks. A subsidiary of Watney Mann & Truman. Mild and bitter. 288 tied houses and only about 30 serve cask.

**Charles Wells:** Bedford. Two bitters. 91 of the 265 tied houses serve cask.

 **Welsh:** Cardiff. A subsidiary of Bass Charrington. Three bitters and two milds. Half the 605 tied houses serve cask.

**Westcrown:** Newark, Notts. One cask bitter. No tied pubs, serving to the free trade.

 **Whitbread:** Breweries in Durham, Cheltenham, Faversham, Leeds, Liverpool, Luton, Marlow, Portsmouth, Romsey, Salford, Samlesbury, Sheffield, Tiverton and Wateringbury. 7,700 tied houses, most serving keg and top pressure beer, but a few of the breweries brew cask: Castle Eden, Durham, has one bitter; Cheltenham one bitter; Marlow two bitters, a mild and an old ale; Portsmouth two bitters and a mild; Romsey mild and bitter; Tiverton two bitters. Salford and Liverpool will introduce cask beers in 1978.

 **Wilsons:** a subsidiary of Watney Mann & Truman, Manchester. Two bitters and a mild. 720 tied houses, 450 with cask.

**Yates and Jackson:** Lancaster. Mild and bitter. 43 tied houses, all with cask.

**York:** York Brewery, York. One bottled beer available only at the brewery/shop.

**Young:** Wandsworth, London SW 18. Two bitters, a mild and an old ale. 135 tied houses, all with cask.

 **Younger:** Edinburgh. A subsidiary of Scottish and Newcastle. Nearly all processed beer. Two cask bitters are available in a few tied outlets and in the free trade.

*Licensing hours: Pub hours vary from district to district but most pubs can open during the hours of 10 to 3 and 5 to 11 although many open later and close earlier. In England and Wales, Sunday opening hours are standard: 12 noon to 2 and 7 to 10.30, except for a few areas of Wales that are dry all day on Sunday. In Scotland, licensing hours have been liberalised in recent years. Weekday hours are 11 to 2.30 and 5 to 11, though many shut earlier in the evening. Hotels are open on Sundays from 12.30 to 2.30 and 6.30 to 10 and pubs may also open on Sundays now if they get permission from the licensing authorities.*

# Index

127